The Moon in Astrology

The Ultimate Guide to Moon Magic, Lunar Phases, and What Your Zodiac Sign Says About You

Your Free Gift (only available for a limited time)

Thanks for getting this book! If you want to learn more about various spirituality topics, then join Mari Silva's community and get a free guided meditation MP3 for awakening your third eye. This guided meditation mp3 is designed to open and strengthen ones third eye so you can experience a higher state of consciousness. Simply visit the link below the image to get started.

https://spiritualityspot.com/meditation

Contents

Introduction

Despite having reached and walked on it, humankind is still fascinated by the amazing celestial body of the Moon. Ever since the dawn of cognizance, the Moon has been a subject of interest and curiosity. While the relative movement and position of the celestial body can determine the natural forces on the Earth, the Moon's power also describes a person's emotions and consciousness. It enables people to find their true purpose, live in harmony with others, and evoke the emotions needed to lead a peaceful life. The celestial body rotates close to Earth and illuminates the surface to strike a balance between utter darkness and brightness.

Despite being smaller than other planets, the power and the gravitational pull of the Moon have stirred interest and curiosity for ages. Past and present-day astronomers use a geocentric approach to decipher natal charts, with the Sun and Moon being significant parts of the readings. The Moon lacks atmosphere, which makes it susceptible to hard rocks, meteor attacks, and an accumulation of debris. However, it can keep its surface free and devoid of wind which keeps its surface intact and prevents significant changes. One can draw this comparison with a person's soul and outer influences. In a way, the Moon symbolizes the need to remold your soul and emotions to avoid exposure to outer chaos.

In astrology, the Moon is a feminine symbol, with the Sun being its counterpart. Collectively, they are vital to the existence of all living creatures, and they monitor and control the natural forces on Earth. Being the feminine entity, the Moon governs our inner child and teaches it to feel safer and more secure in life. She symbolizes fertility, repressed memories, and intuition. A person's astrological chart carries the Moon sign based on the body's position and movement. Since the Moon moves at a fast pace, a few hours can drastically affect a person's fate and bring significant differences in birth charts.

In essence, the Moon covers the entire zodiac wheel in just a month's time, which also characterizes our present-day calendar. The Moon's rapid movement imposes the need to read and pinpoint the exact time of a person's birth. While your Sun sign determines your outer personality and life in general, your Moon sign represents your impulses and emotions. They signify the need to control your emotions and unlock your inner awareness to achieve more stability in life.

If you have been struggling to cope with your emotions lately, consider deciphering your emotions and intuition. By learning more about your Moon sign and its position in your natal chart, you can have better control of your life. This book will elucidate on the spiritual and mythological effects of the Moon and explain its role in your astrological chart. You will learn about the lunar phases and nodes to understand various Moon signs in depth. Furthermore, you will also learn the right way to tap into this celestial body's energy to reap maximum benefits and get your life back on track.

Whether you are seeking knowledge of the Moon signs and the body's significance in your birth chart or are simply curious about astrology and its distinct faces, this book will help you by providing all the information you need. It is easy to read and understand, which ideally makes it a perfect guide for beginners just taking their first steps into astrology. Upon grasping the concept of the Moon sign in its entirety, you will successfully prevent your inner child from repeating the same mistakes, and you can channel your emotions in the right direction.

If you are intrigued and want to learn more about the Moon's role in astrology, then this is the right book for you.

Chapter 1: The Moon as a Goddess

Primarily perceived as a celestial body prompting the solar system's behavior and controlling the tides, the Moon has also been considered a cultural, mythological, and spiritual symbol for centuries. Certain characteristics like immortality, femininity, enlightenment, and eternity are closely associated with it. In the past, the Moon was worshiped as a holy element, and the deity was believed to be a goddess representing fertility and growth. The mythological ties and spiritual affinity with the Moon are associated with the beliefs formed in the past.

Mythological and Spiritual Aspects of the Moon

Being the graceful goddess of luminescence and fertility, the Moon has been perceived as a deity for many years and carries mythological and spiritual connotations in many religions. This celestial body that moves in circles and controls lunar cycles also governs the cycle and rhythm of time. Ancient scholars examined the movement and position of the Moon to track time and determine the fate of newborn babies. While some religions and cultures follow the Sun's path to design their calendars and follow their beliefs in chronological order, others still monitor the lunar cycle to date.

The Moon has also invoked the curiosity of traditional and modern astronomers and astrologers, which is why the celestial body is an important part of natal charts. The Moon's brightness and luminescent nature give mortals hope. The radiance is symbolized as awareness and enlightenment that influences people to seek truth and find their true purpose. The Moon, the Sun, and the stars are manifestations of wisdom and worldly knowledge. They speak to you and deliver musings that not all can decipher. However, if you understand the nature of the Prophets and Luminaries (the archetypes of the celestial bodies), you can achieve divinity and righteousness.

The Moon and the Sun thrive in harmony. Just like they create an even balance between day and night, dark and light, and yin and yang, fasting and prayer, they can develop synergy and induce spiritual growth. The Sun is the Moon's patron. Without its light, the Moon fails to shine brightly and spread brightness on Earth.

Typically, a lunar cycle is counted as a 29.5-day loop, aligning with a woman's menstrual cycle. The words "moon" and "menstruation" share linguistic roots. This, in turn, helped women across many civilizations to keep track of their menstrual cycles.

The Moon's Significance across Civilizations

The Moon has intrigued several civilizations from the dawn of time. Many ancient scholars and poets were fascinated by the peculiar nature of this celestial body and often drew parallels between the Moon Goddess or God and their counterparts. The body's bizarre and fascinating glow led ancient philosophers and scholars to discover its supernatural implications. Every culture and civilization shaped its own version of the Moon deity. While the Greeks called their Moon Goddess Selene, the Egyptians addressed their Lunar God as Thoth. Similarly, other cultures and religions drew implications of their own beliefs and illustrated distinct versions of the Lunar God and Goddess, who stem from similar convictions.

The Moon was considered a noble, natural body that supervised the welfare of mere mortals. On the flip side, some accounts portrayed the Moon as a darker force that led to negative behavior in humans. Whenever a full moon was spotted, the association between criminal acts and lunacy was put forward as being caused by this natural phenomenon. Some storytellers even formulated the idea of werewolves that became more active during full moon nights, thereby causing harm and spreading havoc. These negative implications linked to the Moon were a significant part of European cultures and civilizations. The prominence of lunar eclipses and bad omens further connotes the dark side of some versions of the Moon.

Some Western cultures also spread the story of a man's face on the Moon, which has become a popular tale narrated in schools to this day. While some ancient researchers claimed that the Moon had a perfectly round and smooth surface, others argued that the body possessed a dark and rocky surface.

Lunar Deities across Various Cultures

The Moon Goddess was perceived in different forms across various cultures and religions. While some versions shared similar attributes, others were quite distinct.

Luna in Roman Mythology

Luna is the sister of Sol, the Sun God, and is deemed his female counterpart. Even though they represent the distinct characteristics of day and night, they thrive in harmony and are pretty significant in Roman mythology. Luna was one of the prime goddesses in the "diva triformis" (the three goddesses), a trinity that included Hecate and Proserpina. Collectively, they represent childhood, motherhood, womanhood, old age, and marriage. While some records state that Luna was called Juno and Diana, others address them as the Moon

Goddesses. Luna's image is associated with a crescent moon and a chariot. Her main illustration represents Luna standing while riding the chariot.

She often rides the chariot to cross the sky, moving across the horizon that symbolizes the completion of a night and the start of a new day. Luna symbolizes agriculture and fertility as farmers needed protection from moonlight and dark nights to encourage healthy crop growth. This symbolism makes Luna a primordial fertility goddess, and she plays a significant part in Varro's list of essential deities. Luna was widely worshipped by the Romans, who made dedicated altars and temples for the goddess. Her main temple was set atop the Aventine Hill, which was later destroyed by a fire.

Despite being inferior to other gods, Luna was still popular among her devotees and enjoyed the sacrifices and offerings made for her. Some even compare her to the Greek Moon Goddess, Selene, and deem them the same. Ancient Romans claimed Luna to be Selene's Romanized version and started worshipping her. However, unlike Selene, Luna supposedly shares many attributes with the Romans, which made her stand out and become well-respected. Luna's two-yoke chariot is called "Biga," associated with horses or other animals that act as the main carriers. Some illustrations portray her with two oxen pulling the chariot.

Selene in Greek Mythology

Selene, the Titan Goddess, was one of the most important deities of the ancient Greeks and is still known as the Moon Goddess. Ancient poets and scholars exemplified her as a beautiful version of the moon, after which she became a recurring figure in Greek mythology. She is illustrated as a chariot rider with winged steeds and a crescent-shaped crown on her head. Some records depict her wearing a shining cloak while riding a horse. She was the daughter of Theia (Euryphessa) and Hyperion (The Titan Light God) and the lover of Endymion (the shepherd prince).

Zeus was pleased with Endymion and blessed him with eternal youth. Some stories claim Pan and Zeus to be Selene's lovers. The God Sun, Helios was Selene's sibling, and the brother-sister duo was worshipped as the sun and the moon, respectively. They worked in harmony and audited the movements of the celestial bodies to govern day and nighttime. Ancient Greeks regarded both figures as significant deities as they brought balance to their lives and always monitored the well-being of humans. According to a myth, Selene and Endymion birthed fifty daughters who represented the fifty forms of lunar months. Collectively, the daughters were called the "Menai."

Other records claim that Helios and Selene were, in fact, lovers and gave birth to the four-season goddesses, the Horai. The stories that claim that Zeus and Selene were lovers explain the birth of Dionysus, who represented theater and wine. Selene is known to travel across the sky on her chariot with her white horses. As she travels, she leaves a trail of silvery light that provides enough light to the living beings on Earth. At the same time, she keeps an eye on them and looks after their sleep.

Chang'e in Chinese Mythology

The East Asian version of the Moon Goddess, Chang'e, is a significant part of Chinese folklore and appears in many accounts. The deity's tale is associated with betrayal and sacrifice. Chang is the goddess's actual name, and the suffix "e" refers to a young and beautiful woman. Older stories address the Moon Goddess as Heng'e. However, it is believed that the ruler, Lui Heng disliked the idea of sharing his name with anyone, which is why they referred to the goddess as Chang'e. Despite the name change, the worshippers were devoted to the goddess and made several sacrifices in her name.

She was believed to be a young, beautiful girl working under the Jade Emperor at his palace in heaven. Chang'e resided with fairies and immortals in the palace and lived a peaceful life. However, her peace was disturbed since the day she broke an expensive and unique porcelain jar. She was banished from the Empire and sent to Earth to live with other mortal beings. Only by contributing to a noble service or valuable cause on Earth could she be allowed to return to heaven. As she began living with a low-income family, Hou Yi, a young hunter, befriended Chang'e, and they started spending a lot of time together, and they eventually grew fond of each other. According to a popular legend, Hou Yi saved Earth from the blaring heat spread by ten suns as he shot down 9 of them.

As a token of admiration, Emperor Lao gifted him an elixir of immortality that Chang'e ended up drinking. She ran towards the moon and floated in the sky to keep a distance from her husband, Hou Yi. However, he chased her and tried to stop her from fleeing by shooting arrows towards the moon. He missed his shot, and Chang'e disappeared into the sky. To date, she is associated with the Moon Goddess, and the couple symbolizes yin and yang.

While the female Lunar deities are well-known across various religions and cultures, the male Lunar figures are also a significant part of the mythological lore. Even though some male deities barely possess lunar aspects, they are still significant to their cultures due to their symbolization.

Chandra in Hindu Mythology

Chandra, or "Chandrasekhar," is the alleged eighth incarnation of Lord Shiva, who was a vital part of the Hindu Trinity- Brahma, Vishnu, and Mahesh. He is represented with long, luscious locks on his head and a half-crescent moon depicting his name. His name translates to "as bright as the moon," which portrays his beautiful image on his marriage day. In essence, Chandrasekhar is known to be Lord Shiva's most beautiful incarnation or version to date, where he shines and glows. Chandra literally means *Moon* and symbolizes emotions, senses, and wisdom. Faithful devotees often receive blessings in the form of a healthy and disease-free life.

Chandra possesses the nectar of the Gods, also known as Soma, and uses it to grow plants and put life into vegetation. He also controls the water waves and tides in deep seas and oceans, making him the legislator of nourishment and fertility. In the past, Indian women were encouraged to fast on Mondays to please the Moon God and find a suitable partner. This tradition still exists in some parts of India.

He thrives in the northwest direction and represents the Cancer constellation. According to a myth, Chandra was born from Arth Rishi's tears of joy. The Moon God in Hindu mythology is portrayed as a slim and tall deity with kind eyes and polite speech. His aura is infectious, and his demeanor makes one seek inner peace. He holds a lotus in one hand and is driven around in a chariot pulled by ten horses.

Sin in Mesopotamian Mythology

Sin, or Nanna, is a lunar deity of the ancient Mesopotamian or Sumerian people. Even though the Moon God was primarily worshipped in the city of Ur, devotion to him spread across the rest of the region after he was considered a significant deity. Today, you can still find several temples spread across the region, supposedly dedicated to the Moon God. Sin represents a bull and is deeply associated with cattle.

Just like the distinct phases of a menstrual cycle in a woman's body, the different versions of the moon during a cycle signify the deity's association with fertility. Enlil, the Sky God, fell in love with Ninlil, the Goddess of grain, and they gave birth to Sin. The Moon God's influence on the Mesopotamian people grew, and they started designing their calendars based on the moon's direction and the lunar cycle.

While Sin was illustrated as a half-moon, Nanna was portrayed as the new or full moon. The deity's symbol, the bull, was also associated with the moon's crescent shape. Nanna wears a crown resembling a moon disk and is called "Lord of the Diadem." Nanna is extremely wise and helps those who are confused or are seeking knowledge. Priests, mortals, and other gods also visited Nanna to gain advice. Sin is a part of the holy triad of the ancient Mesopotamian religion, which comprises Ishtar (Venus), Shamash (Sun), and Sin.

Thoth in Egyptian Mythology

Thoth was essentially associated with the Ibis bird of wisdom, as he possessed immense knowledge and wisdom on several topics. Ra, the Sun God, was always fascinated by Thoth's wisdom and appointed him as his personal advisor. His knowledge and personal attributes were often compared to the Greek God, Hermes. Thoth was a significant deity in ancient Egypt, especially in agriculture and astronomy. Some myths claim the Moon God to be Set and Horus's son who was conceived during battle. Other myths tell of Thoth's peculiar birth event where he appeared from Set's forehead.

The Moon God has several depictions and is illustrated in various lights in Egyptian mythology. Other accounts claim that the god is Ra's son and that he fathered Thoth from his lips. Ra was the Moon God's only parent, which is why he was labeled as "the god without a mother." The story behind Thoth's existence and predominance is associated with his symbolization of the Ibis. It says that Thoth was, in fact, the Ibis, and he created life on Earth by laying a cosmic egg.

Thoth has three wives who are also significant to ancient Egyptian religion. While the goddess of balance and truth, Ma'at, is Thoth's principal wife, some even claim Seshat (the Goddess of Books and Writing) and Nehmetawy (The Goddess of Safety and Protection) to be his dominant partners. Thoth symbolized a crescent moon and played a vital role as the Moon God in the past. He is also closely associated with a specter, stylus, scales, and a papyrus scroll.

The Moon's Spiritual Importance in Today's Time

Over time, as humans got more curious and delved deeper into scientific research and studies, their perception of the Moon steadily shifted from a mystical power to a dry wasteland. However, certain cultures still believe that the position and relevance of the Moon determine their fate. Ancient beliefs – merged with present-day astrological readings – have spurred modern spiritual denotation of this celestial body. Since it takes around a month to form a new moon, the modern way of following time shows implications from the past. Today, one can hardly deny that the Moon's energy and synergy are sending messages and vibrations that possess the power to manipulate our thoughts, emotions, and feelings. In fact, these manifestations can also affect the people around us.

The changes in tides and oceans are caused by the Moon's gravitational pull, especially during the Full and New Moon day. One can say that a person's body, which is mainly made up of water, is also controlled by the Moon's movement. Humans tend to feel more emotional or experience a surge in their emotions on prime days, which are specifically apparent on a Full Moon.

In a way, the Moon's movement and phases also affect the Earth's frequency and magnetic field due to salty water in oceans and fluctuating water levels. These changes affect not only our brain's cognitive capacity but also our sleep and brain wave performance. As you can see, the Moon's mystical power can lead to significant changes in our body, mind, and soul. Specific modern-day techniques are being implemented to manifest positive changes in humans during different phases of the Moon. For instance, certain self-care strategies can help a person feel more at ease on a New Moon.

While the Sun defines our outer personality and extroverted nature, the Moon signifies unconscious thoughts and beliefs, which can be effectively remolded for better outcomes. If you learn the right way to unlock the mystical nature of the Moon, you will be blessed with abundance and creativity.

Its Role in Modern Witchcraft and Wicca

Modern witchcraft and Wicca magic are still being practiced in some regions, and the Moon is the central element of every reading.

A Lunar cycle is completed over the course of around 27 days. The different phases of the Moon, including the waxing and waning, are studied to attract positivity. Specific rituals are performed to access the Moon's spiritual energy and harness its power.

If you are successful, you can easily reach your goals. While the Moon's waxing phase is used to attract positivity, the Moon's waning phase is used to send negativity or any unwanted object out of your life. The Full Moon phase is the most fruitful event of all phases, and it is marked as the "harvest" season.

Not all magicians and witches prefer to work on Dark Moon days as it may have negative repercussions. On a positive note, one can perform magic on a Dark Moon day to rewind, refresh, and bring closure to complete the circle.

Chapter 2: The Moon in Astrology

The mythological and spiritual implications of the Moon lead to its significance and relevance in the world of astrology. It impacts the emotional and spiritual well-being of every individual in one way or another. While several Western cultures perform their astrological readings using the Sun signs, Hindu culture designs their natal charts based on individual Moon signs. In the past, Hindus based their birth dates according to the Moon's position and relevant signs. The birth date was marked as the day when the sign overlapped with Moon's entrance. However, after the British established their base in India, people celebrated their birthdays based on the calendar dates.

The Moon's Astrological Significance

When a person is born, their natal chart includes the Moon's position and behavior to determine their fate. Lagna, or the ascendant in the horoscope, is a respected and influential house. The involvement of the Moon in this house makes it the Chandra Lagna, which is used to determine *a person's fate* when they are born. The Moon influences the Cancer sign and is associated with other planets in a clockwise direction.

It takes around 324 days to orbit around all zodiac signs, thereby becoming a part of each sign for several days (around 27 days) throughout the year. The Moon governs the fourth sign and Cancer's fourth house. You can study the astrological implications of this celestial body by examining its conjunction with other planets, day of the week, color, body parts, emotions and values, constellations, emotional health, and professions.

Day and Color

In astrology, the Moon is associated with Monday and the color white. Some claim that the word "Monday" was derived from "Moon."

The shadowy and emotional demeanor of the Moon resembles the first day of the week, which often feels intuitive and moody. At times, taking the first step can feel quite challenging. Like the New Moon (the first phase of a lunar cycle), Mondays can feel overwhelming. However, as the days pass, you get comfortable with the flow. This allocation of the week's first day can be dated back to the Babylonians' time when ancient scholars divided a lunar cycle into four quarters. The implication is that the first day was linked to the Moon's first phase of birth. As mentioned, Hindu women fasted on Mondays to please Chandra and attract suitable partners for marriage.

Since the Moon's surface is white and bright, this hue is quite significant to the planet. The cosmic rays, energy fields, and the Moon's aura are represented by white. This hue is made from the seven colors of the spectrum, thereby making it the purest shade of all. It motivates people to gather inspiration from their surroundings and take the spiritual path. In the past, devotees dedicated white flowers and objects to the Moon. Typically, white jasmines, lotuses, and lilies were associated with the Moon Goddess. Objects like white sandalwood, curd, milk, and rice flour were also considered sacred. However, astrologers refrain from using too much white as it can reverse the positive effects.

Other Planets

The Moon is friendly with Jupitei and Mars as all three thrive in harmony. When these planets align together, the person may be blessed with immense luck or mental peace. Astrologers consider this association to be optimistic. On the other hand, it fails to create a healthy connection with Saturn, Ketu, and Rahu. Furthermore, it keeps a safe distance from Mercury as both share a neutral relationship that is neither imperial nor hideous. However, if Mercury starts dominating the Moon, the person is susceptible to neurological disorders. Even though the Moon is neutral and tries to be fair to all, its union with other planets determines the body's status. If the other planet is regressive, it can negatively affect your mental and emotional health.

Despite sharing a strong bond with the Sun, the correlation does not bring much to the table. Collectively, they represent confidence and ambition. The Venus-Moon pair symbolizes love and romantic relationships. If this combination is prominent in your astrological chart, consider taking a creative profession like music production or fashion design, as you will likely succeed in your career. If the Moon's pertinence is strong with Rahu or Ketu, you can suffer from financial loss or mental health issues. A steady balance between these two planets can mean liberation or enlightenment.

Emotions and Values

The Moon is peaceful and calm by nature and inspires others to seek solitude by regaining consciousness and self-awareness. It symbolizes emotions, imaginative power, the importance of being or having a mother, mental stability, prosperity, wisdom, peace of mind, and trading. It is feminine by nature and thrives at a low temperature. The Moon can be very fruitful or extremely negative depending on the position and phase. A well-placed planet depicts a healthy relationship with your parents, especially your mother, and a supportive family. You are blessed with a healthy mind and emotional availability. You have immense wealth and a big house where you are at peace and able to live comfortably.

The Full Moon, which also stands at the highest order of a lunar cycle, brings joy to one's life, and it is regarded as beneficial. On the other hand, the New Moon, which is basically non-existent, is perceived as malefic. If the Full Moon overlaps with your zodiac sign, you will likely gain wisdom or be blessed with creativity. In essence, the Moon represents every feminine aspect of living beings and the universe. Beauty, happiness, eyesight, well-being, mind, and memory are some of the other attributes presented by this orbiting energy.

Constellations

The planet is associated with the Sravana, Hasta, and Rohini constellations (also known as "Nakshatra"). As the Moon orbits the Earth and takes around 27 days to complete a cycle, it also covers the 27 Nakshatras or Lunar Mansions during this period. Typically, the Moon enters, stays, and exits one Nakshatra every day. Your Moon Nakshatra significantly influences your self-awareness and consciousness, which is why you should learn more about your constellation. Other constellations that blend well with the Moon's energy include Vishaka, Punarvasu, and Purva Bhadrapad. In other constellations like Uttra Khad, Kritika, Ashlekha, Uttara Phalguni, Revati, and Jyestha, the amalgamation results in neutral to favorable outcomes.

Every lunar mansion is supervised by one planet – each distinct in both nature and characteristics. As the Moon enters different mansions every day, your birthday will be marked based on its position. This mansion or constellation will be marked as your Moon Nakshatra. While the Moon's energy is solely powerful, its symbiosis with respective Nakshatras makes it even more authoritative. By successfully deciphering your Moon Nakshatra, you can unravel your life's purpose and hidden intricacies, which will attract success and emotional well-being – the right path towards self-discovery and fighting inner conflicts.

Gemstone

It represents the gemstone, pearl, which is also white. A pearl enhances a woman's physical appearance and makes her look more beautiful, which is also a symbolism portrayed by the Moon. Furthermore, a pearl represents depth and awareness, which also aligns with the Moon's values. It is believed that a person who wears a real pearl daily can attract fame and appreciation over time. In some cases, wearing this gemstone can also alleviate certain physical health symptoms related to cough, cold, bronchitis, throat issues, hysteria, eye diseases, typhoid, varicose veins, tumors, and intestinal disorders, among many others.

You can either place a pearl near your bedside or wear it as a pendant or a ring. Astrologers suggest wearing a pearl weighing between 1200 to 1400 mg. You can also pick a pearl with more weight. If you are wearing it as a ring, put it on your dominant hand's little finger so that it makes contact with your skin. Hindu astrologers suggest dipping the pearl in holy water for 10 to 15 minutes before wearing it. To achieve more favorable outcomes, wait for the next Monday to arrive before you put it on your finger. When wearing it, chant the mantra, "OM CHANDRAYA NAMAH." Use a soft brush and soapy water to clean the pearl from time to time, as accumulated dust can reduce its positive effects.

The Moon also symbolizes the hare. While some of the stories associated a hare with the Moon, the significance can be drawn from the steadiness of this animal. Just like a hare jumps and leaps around at a fast pace, the Moon also moves faster than other planets. Vedic lore depicts the Moon as a rabbit because it steadily leaps and hops from one place to another without resting at one spot for long.

Metal

It represents metal and silver. While some may argue that the bright, silvery illumination is the basic correlation of this metal with the celestial body, astrologers claim that the purifying properties of silver align with the Moon's cleansing nature. When you think of moonlight over a silent lake, you can imagine a clear, silver palette shining over the water surface. It looks like liquid silver with mysterious properties. It helps release stress and encourages you to explore the beauty of nature, much like the Moon itself. Metal is related to sensuality, femininity, and connectivity. Silver also exemplifies the properties of minerals and gemstones attached to it, thereby making the effects even more potent.

Body Parts

The Moon firmly signifies motherhood and fertility. Certain body parts like the heart, eyes, bodily fluids, and lungs are also associated with it. In essence, it also governs women's breasts and lactation during childbirth. Vedic astrology believes that the Moon rules a person's left eye and nostril. If the Moon enters an unfavorable mansion or transits into a hostile state, you may likely face issues around any of these body parts. While minor cases include sleeplessness and fatigue, some may suffer from adverse health conditions like asthma.

Emotional, Mental, and Physical Health

If the celestial body is placed in a weak position, the person will likely suffer from respiratory issues, cardiac problems, weak eyesight, cold, or depression. On the other hand, a well-placed planet portrays better physical and mental health along with strong imagination and intelligence. If the Moon rules in your favor, you can implement certain effective strategies like meditation to combat physical problems and enhance your mental power.

Profession

The Moon supports professions like fishing, water trading, sailing, pearl trading, gynecology, or dairy farming. Since the Moon represents motherhood, gynecology can be a rewarding profession for ambitious people.

The Moon and Its Ruler, Cancer

While the Sun rules the Leo sign, the Moon looks over those under the sign of Cancer. Since it is a Water sign, Cancer dominates a person's spiritual and emotional side. When combined with the lunar attributes, individuals born under this zodiac sign possess strong emotions and are more attuned to their feelings. They are self-aware and can empathize with others. The lunar waxing and waning nature emphasize the recurring changes and cyclical patterns associated with the Moon. When compared to Cancer's attributes, people may likely display cyclical behavior too.

While your own emotions govern your condition, your mood may also change or become influenced by the distinct energies around you. At times, these situations can make it more difficult to accept changes and adapt to new environments, affecting you emotionally and mentally. You must develop skills to take control of your life and emotions. If you are successful, you will likely have optimum emotional balance. In some cases, the Moon may inspire you to take a more traditional approach and be deeply involved with your family and loved ones. If you are experiencing similar nurturing or protective feelings, remember to give space to your loved ones while you take care of them.

While Scorpio debilitates the Moon and reduces its positive impact, Taurus elevates the celestial body and promotes better outcomes.

The Moon and Scorpio

While the association of the Moon with this zodiac sign is already grim, the former's position and affiliation with an ominous planet can negatively impact a person's fate. This cooperation is often perceived as a bad omen by astrologers. In this case, the Moon is extremely weak and can also be destructive in some cases. As mentioned, if this version of the planet aligns with Saturn, Ketu, or Rahu, it can result in severe mental issues like forgetfulness, obsessive-compulsive disorder, poor decision-making skills, migraine, or depression.

The Moon and Taurus

Unlike Scorpio that debilitates the Moon, the Tarusu supports and enhances it. Since this zodiac sign works well with the Moon, it empowers a person's fate when they are born. This version of the white celestial body is extremely powerful. The person is blessed with immense creativity and a strong mind. They possess impressive imaginary skills as well. Furthermore, the Moon's power is also tested according to the house it is placed in. If it is placed in Kendra with the 7th house, it makes one of the most powerful versions of the Moon.

How to Strengthen a Debilitated Moon

Fortunately, you can implement certain tips to strengthen a debilitated moon and turn the results in your favor.

Donate Wisely

Individuals with a weak Moon should refrain from accepting silver in any form. Whether it's a reward or a donation, do not accept silver. However, you can demand silver in the form of jewelry from your mother and wear it as a chain. Some other objects significant to the Moon are milk, white flowers, and crystals. It is believed that donating milk can also bring a positive change.

On the other hand, you can donate silver to those in need. Since real silver can be pretty expensive, astrologers suggest donating a single silver thread as it is more affordable. Donations shouldn't be announced to the world. Keep it to yourself and just accept the gratitude from the ones receiving it. Do not feel proud or egoistic when donating something and try to forget it. Note that the Moon supports humility and modesty. It is important to stay grounded.

Try Visualization Techniques

Certain visualization techniques are not only useful for your mental peace and spiritual growth, but they also strengthen your Moon's position. In essence, they activate your Third Eye or Ajna chakra that deliberately flushes out negativity from your system. This, in turn, helps make room for positive thoughts and manifests better outcomes. Performing visualization techniques also helps you channel your emotions and attract happiness. The idea is to think of a positive outcome and believe that you have already achieved your goal; while it may seem useless, it works.

Basically, by thinking that you have overcome your current problem, you manifest the Moon's and the universe's energies to experience it in real life. Since it can be challenging to concentrate and visualize your outcomes, practice meditation to improve concentration. Along with performing visualization techniques, you can also practice breathing techniques like Anulom-Vilom and Diaphragmatic Breathing.

Wear the Moon's Gemstone and Metal

As mentioned earlier, wearing an authentic white pearl can strengthen a debilitated moon and help you stay attuned to the Moon's energy. To further strengthen its power, pair the pearl with a silver necklace or a ring. Since silver represents the Moon and possesses purifying properties, this combination can help cleanse your emotions and soul. You can also get a necklace made with real silver and a white pearl as its pendant. Remember that the necklace or ring should always stay in contact with your skin.

You can also get an auspicious showpiece made of real silver and place it on your mantle or bedside. Keep it clean and dust-free to unravel its maximum power. Some other objects you can keep in your house to strengthen your Moon include peacock feathers, small plants, and silver "supari." The plants should face north if you can, fast on Mondays, and eat healthy during the rest of the week.

Conduct a "Shanti Kriya"

This kriya or ritual is based on psychic energy and enables the forces to divert the Moon's positive energy in your favor. It involves a holy ritual with tantras and meditation exercises. The priest or astrologer performs the kriya chants, a series of powerful mantras to induce positive vibrations and make the ritual more successful. While taking help from an astrologer can help you achieve better results, you can also learn some mantras and chant them on Mondays while performing the kriyas. For instance, the Prarthana mantra, Avahan mantra, and Chintan or Chandra Dhyan mantra are used to ward off negative energies and bring more positivity.

You can make a few minor changes in your daily life like wearing white clothes, eating white foods like rice, coconut, and kheer, meditating and chanting mantras on Mondays, and using crystals for internal healing. Note that these rituals and actions can take some time to show a positive outcome. You must be patient and believe in the process.

Some of these techniques and rituals will also be discussed and elaborated on in the last chapter, which considers some effective ways to strengthen a weak Moon.

Even though the Moon sign is not as popular as the Sun sign, it is still considered an important celestial body in Vedic astrology. The Moon is now considered to be the most powerful and important natural body in this domain.

Note that the accuracy of the Moon's position and orbiting energy must be calculated with precision. An inexperienced astrologer may draw inaccurate results, thereby damaging your birth chart. It is crucial to find a wise and experienced astrologer who can perform meticulous calculations and make an accurate birth chart. They will also advise you on the right way to combat stress or other mental health issues based on your condition by computing the Moon's position and its association with other planets.

Chapter 3: Your Moon Signs I

Your moon sign is directly related to your emotional energy. It indicates your personality and innate reactions, and it highlights what you need to feel more secure. Your moon sign shines a light on your emotional state and intuition.

Aries Moon Sign

Aries is a cardinal fire sign; when you are born with the moon in Aries, there is likely a very strong need for independence. You are also likely to be very assertive. You will feel your best when you are dealing with things that are exciting and challenging. These challenging experiences bring you immense joy. New experiences allow you to bring out your innovative side.

Characteristic Traits

Aries often indicates emotional independence. You might find that you put in your time, effort, and energy, expecting the same in return. You are, however, quick to forgive but are easily hurt. You will often find yourself chasing freedom and alone time. Although you give to others, this need for solitude is important for you to recalibrate and get a sense of your own self. Feeling pressured or controlled by others dampens your spirits and your innate need for independence.

A cardinal sign is a front-runner in the zodiac signs. They are go-getters, dynamic, and incredibly powerful. As a cardinal sign, there is often a need and deep desire to act. You may find that you like to get things going, and you don't take a back seat. You always try to move things forward and set them in motion.

Strengths

You are very likely a straight-talker, and you don't feel the need to hide your feelings or thoughts with niceties. Instead, you prefer to be upfront, and you tend to deal with things directly and clearly. You have this warrior-like sense that allows you to deal with hardships efficiently. Because of that, you may find that you often expect others to do the same.

You are often able to intuitively draw on the internal resources you need in a time of need. Often, when you have a goal in mind, you can speed toward it completely focused. You can easily remove all distractions that keep you from your goal. Your moon in Aries gives you the necessary focus and internal resources needed to thrive. Because you move quickly and focus, others are easily left behind when you concentrate on what you want.

Aries moons tend to be extroverted and love attention from others. Your emotional reactions may be big displays that capture the attention of others. If you are happy, your happiness is displayed loud and proud. If you cry, you tend to cry your eyes out. You express your emotions in an incredibly intense way. People may want to get to know you because of the way you present yourself.

Weaknesses

A weakness of this placement is that you might find yourself making decisions based on your first instinctive feelings. You find yourself rushing in, and this leads to errors of judgment. To avoid this, you should learn how other people feel and think and make your decisions accordingly. Don't feel the need to ignore your instincts, but instead, use this alongside a good understanding of the situation in front of you to make the best possible decision.

Another weakness you could exhibit is impatience. You may want everything to come easily, and you expect others to move as quickly as you do, leading to constantly getting annoyed – or even outbursts of anger. To deal with this and to avoid getting irritated by how slow something is progressing, be realistic. Realize that not everything can happen with the snap of a finger. It takes time for goals to actualize and become a reality.

Taurus Moon Sign

Those who have their moon in Taurus are often calm, mellow, and grounded. The moon and Taurus go hand in hand, and this is an easy and relaxed fit. You are grounded in your body, as opposed to being so consumed by the thoughts in your head. In this modern world, it is hard to find people who are grounded. The rush of our lifestyles has meant that many have retreated to the safety of their minds, limiting them from enjoying the wonder and joy of everyday life. It may mean that they make mistakes and live in a place of fear, and are consumed with meaningless thoughts.

Characteristic Traits

With the moon in Taurus, you are much better equipped to handle the world around you calmly. You may notice that you deal with things at a slower pace compared to others because you have the advantage of being grounded in the present. You love to focus on the small joys of life.

Strengths

Taurus is a fixed sign that means you can easily put all your energy into one thing and complete it well. Pair that with your innately grounded nature, and you may find that you can make great strides in your hobbies. The moon in Taurus will actually help you find your hobbies and discover your talents easily.

Your patient nature gives you the necessary time and energy to allow you to immerse yourself in whatever you want or need. You find yourself craving stability more than anything. You may seek situations and partners that allow you to feel complete comfort, security, and stability.

However, a drawback to this desire for stability is that it may make you rigid and unwilling to change. If you are unaware that you have innate patience, a need for stability, and being grounded, it can easily turn into laziness.

Weaknesses

Because you are so attached to your routines and habits, you may hesitate to make big moves or changes that improve or add benefit to your life. You could miss out on important opportunities by deliberating rather than taking action. It is best to become aware of your tendencies and know how you act or think during important phases of your life to combat this. The more aware you become, the easier it will be for you to make a change.

Start taking action. Some fear may arise because it is not in your nature to make decisions quickly. You need to push through that fear. Feel it, process it, and overcome it. Allow yourself to think and reflect and then, once you have all the facts, allow yourself to make a choice that could lead to change.

Often, you may fear change and consider it to be a bad thing. You can easily become stubborn, which, in turn, leads to stagnation in life. Choose instead to make new and bold choices. Get used to overcoming the fear and choose to do something anyway.

Gemini Moon Sign

The air sign of Gemini in your moon may mean that you have an innate thirst for knowledge. You have a deep desire to understand and know as much as you can about the world around you. You are very likely a curious individual with an incredibly active mind.

Characteristic Traits

The underpinning theme of this sign is communication. You may love sharing information and knowledge with others. You could be a very chatty person with a lot to say. You may also have friends from all walks of life and the ability to move around and fit in with all kinds of people. Sharing ideas, information, and knowledge spark joy, allowing you to be friends with different types of people. You feel like you are being true to yourself the most when you are engaged in learning new things.

Strengths

Your mind is often active and constantly taking in and processing information from the world around you, sometimes leading to you feeling overwhelmed – but you may like how often and how fast your mind works.

Gemini is a mutable sign, and there is a need for new stimulation and change. You could find yourself becoming quickly and easily engrossed in new things. Becoming bored easily may be one of your habits, but you are adaptable and a great multi-tasker. Taking on multiple projects and doing several tasks at once often comes naturally to you.

Often, you don't feel the need to study or learn much about something to feel like you know it. You may only need a glimpse to be satisfied. Just like how you can jump from group to group, you can easily jump between ideas, concepts, and facts.

You need to develop the skill of discretion as this will help you avoid getting yourself into any sticky situations.

Your inquisitive nature helps you connect with others. You can easily speak to people about their problems and issues, finding out what makes them tick. You don't care much for their deep emotional problems but rather the oddities of their life issues or circumstances.

Once you have someone figured out, you may feel the need to move on to the next person, no longer interested in what this particular person has to say. It feels as if you have satisfied your need for information, and your desire to get to know other people is genuine. Don't mistake it for anything else. You only think of moving on to the next person because you want to know more people.

The moon is associated with nurturing, and you may find that you can easily make others feel good about themselves with what you have to say. You can nurture others with your words, and you make them feel better.

You may be known for your humor and ability to entertain. It is often easy for you to keep things fun and entertaining. Gemini moons tend to use humor to avoid or release feelings of tension. Do you often find yourself making jokes about things that are emotionally difficult? You find this easier than most and like to use humor to distract yourself and others. Compared to more emotional moon signs, the Gemini moon is more detached, making them seem superficial.

You can easily tread on the surface of situations, with an uncanny ability to keep things light and easy if they start to get a little dark.

Weaknesses

A problem you may run into is that it could be hard for you to feel your emotions. Instead, you find it easier to objectify your experiences and categorize them in a way that detaches you from having to feel anything.

You tend to avoid any deep emotional situations and stick to the rational side of things. You may use logic to deal with a situation as opposed to feeling your emotions. The problem with this is that you may begin to suppress your emotions over long periods, which can cause problems for you in the long run. Your emotions may blow up over minor things, and you may struggle to regulate your emotions.

Begin to tune into your emotions and use them to assess how you truly feel about a situation instead of just relying on your logic. Tuning into this may help you make better decisions based on a more informed understanding of yourself.

Your love for both words and numbers means that you may enjoy the hustle and bustle of trade or retail. Gadgets, tech, and new innovations may excite you.

Cancer Moon Sign

Cancer moons are at home, as the moon rules Cancer. Cancer is a cardinal sign, which means you very likely have a deep desire to take action. Especially when it comes to others, you may feel responsible for both the physical and emotional well-being of others.

Characteristic Traits

You may have a deep need to nurture, and connect with others, especially with your loved ones. Your emotional health often stems from the relationships you have developed with your family. There is an innate desire to support, protect, and nurture.

As the moon rules Cancer, this strengthens the emotional, empathetic, and intuitive aspects. You may find yourself being strongly influenced by your emotions and mood that constantly fluctuates and the moods of others around you.

Strengths

Consider the moon, which is cyclical in nature. Just as the moon wanes and waxes, you, too, are a cyclical being. Your emotions wax and wane just like the moon. Logic and rationality take a backseat for cancer moons. Instead, internal cycles and instincts often take over.

As you learn to get in touch with this natural rhythm, this internal sense of self can be used positively. The more in touch you are, the more you will understand yourself and what you need in each moment. You will be able to follow your internal compass and make decisions and choices that accurately reflect how you feel.

You will thrive and feel your best when you abide by these internal cycles. Because your emotions are ever-changing, it is best if you respect their ebb and flow and avoid sticking to a rigid routine. Allow yourself flexibility, and don't feel bad if you cannot stick to a strict schedule or are not as productive as you want to be every day. It would be better for you to follow your internal wishes, as this is a great signpost to how you should spend your energy that day. Use this to guide you and as a way to see how much more energy you have and how much you can get done.

One way to use this emotional energy in the right way is to take complete accountability for just how sensitive and emotional you are. Perhaps people have told you in a negative manner that you are too emotional or sensitive. Get rid of this shame and allow yourself to celebrate the fact that you are this way. It provides you with gifts that others do not innately have.

Weaknesses

A weakness of being so emotional or sensitive is that you may find yourself significantly affected by the emotional state of other people around you. Their emotions may affect yours, and you may end up carrying around other people's emotions as well as yours. If this is you, learn to differentiate between your emotions and those of others. Take some time to reflect and find the root of the emotion. If it does not belong to you, permit yourself to let it float away. It is easier said than done but, with practice, you will find that you can release yourself from the burden of other people's emotions and maybe even your own.

Cancer moons may find that they are impressionable and often soak up other people's feelings or opinions and make them their own. Because you are so intuitive, you can easily tune into others and how they are feeling at any given moment and then take on both their emotional burdens and attitudes. Become aware of this when you are around others, question the things you think and feel, and ask yourself if it is truly what you think and or if you may have picked it up from somewhere else.

Your emotional sensitivity is like a superpower, but it can cause you to stress out if you do not use it properly. To make the most of it, you must ensure you stay grounded. Stay centered and connected to your body. You can do this through daily meditation, exercise, spending some time alone, or anything that makes you feel relaxed and in control.

Learning to regulate your emotions will provide you with a healthy way to manage your mood. The more it fluctuates, the harder it will be to act and feel in a way that is authentic to yourself. Learn to stay grounded, relaxed, and in the moment. In this way, you can effortlessly process your emotions and learn to discern between which emotions are yours and which are not.

Chapter 4: Your Moon Signs II

The moon's position in the sky affects a person's mood and behavior. It can also influence things like health, appearance, and creativity. The moon is constantly changing its position in the sky, which means that people are always going through different phases of life. The Zodiac signs are divided by their corresponding moon signs to represent these phases of life. Each one has its unique personality traits as well as strengths and weaknesses that you should know about. This chapter will teach you everything there is to know about the Moon Signs Leo, Virgo, Libra, and Scorpio, so you'll never be caught off guard again!

Leo Moon Sign

The Leo moon sign is ruled by the Sun and has a fixed element of Fire. People born under this sign can be passionate about their interests, but they tend to become obsessive. When they get into something, nothing can stop them from doing it right. However, the problem is that few people have the energy and willpower to go through with their plans when they make up their minds; perhaps this isn't something negative, though, because Leos are just very passionate people! They don't worry too much about what happens in life, but they just live it! If you're hanging out with a Leo moon, you must know their characteristics, strengths, and weaknesses.

Characteristic Traits

People with a Leo moon sign are cheerful, friendly, and confident. They enjoy life to the fullest at all times. Often feeling superior to others, they will expect praise for everything they do. If you're working on a project with them, you can expect a completed job well done. They can show true love in the most spectacular way possible, so if they fall for you, it's usually for good. They are self-centered and can be controlling, but they do it with good intentions. They can work up the courage to be vulnerable. People with a Leo moon sign are warm-hearted and generous, especially when they're around the ones that they love. They enjoy comforts of all sorts, so they'll make sure everything is perfect before doing anything else.

Strengths

Leo moon signs have a big heart, which allows them to do anything they put their mind to. They're strong-willed, confident, and creative. They're not afraid to overcome obstacles to get the job done. Their courageous nature can help them to overcome the fear of failure.

They are also very determined and can inspire others to be ambitious and determined as well. If one thing is worth it to them, they won't stop until that thing is completed. Leos are very passionate about life, and it can make them seem like a powerhouse at times. They're often the center of attention wherever they go because they know how to take control of a situation.

Weaknesses

The one flaw with this sign is their need for praise. They don't like to share the spotlight with anyone else, and they can sometimes be very insensitive towards others. If they're not getting enough attention, they may attempt to get it by doing something drastic. They also get angered quite easily, which can lead them to be impatient and inflexible. They have a hard time listening to the opinions of others, so it could cause issues if you're trying to reason with someone who has a Leo moon sign. While they are quite confident, they also tend to be jealous. If you're a Leo, you should always work on being more open-minded and flexible when it comes to interpersonal relationships. You can also try to curb your jealousy and have more confidence in yourself. It will help you become much more likable!

Leos are ruled by the Sun, so they need to be pampered and appreciated. They can do anything if they're motivated enough, but sometimes that motivation isn't there due to a lack of appreciation. If you want a Leo moon sign to do something for you, make sure that it's worth their while. They need to be appreciated for what they do for others, but they also need to know beforehand what's at stake. If you want them to stick around, make sure that they know you're not just taking advantage of their eagerness.

Virgo Moon Sign

The Virgo moon sign is very reliable and practical. They are excellent at helping others get organized, and they have an eye for details. They like working on small projects that require attention to detail, such as puzzles or intricate drawings. People born under this sign naturally love doing things for other people, so you can expect them to be good friends.

You can also expect them to be good conversationalists. Virgo moon signs are very interested in learning new things, and they love to discuss their thoughts with others. If you have something interesting that you want to share, you should look into telling a person born under this sign because the odds are that they will listen intently. They also love to have fun, so you can be sure that they will love any of your jokes and stories.

Characteristic Traits

The Virgo moon sign has many wonderful traits. They are very honest, and they are willing to listen to constructive criticism. These people also love to read, and you can expect them to learn more and more throughout their lives. You can never say that a person born under the Virgo sign doesn't have an eye for detail because they catch every little detail in life. They are very intuitive, and they will always try to help others when they can. If you are trying to organize a group of volunteers, someone with the Virgo moon sign would be an excellent choice. They also enjoy assisting in the community and giving back in any way they can.

People born under the Virgo moon sign are excellent problem solvers. They love to fix things, and they will give you their full attention when you need them most. You can expect these people to help you feel better if you are going through a rough patch in your life or if you have made a mistake. These people also possess many strengths that make them an excellent choice when it comes to jobs. They will always follow the rules and be on time regardless of how much pressure they are under at any given moment.

Strengths

The strengths of the Virgo moon sign include their practical nature, sense of responsibility, and their ability to work with others. If you have a task that requires someone who can follow orders well and work in groups, then this is the person for the job. These people may seem cold and distant on the surface, but they are very sensitive and intelligent deep down, though they may choose not to exhibit that feeling. If you need help organizing your life, this is also a sign that will *be happy to assist you*!

When dealing with a person born under this sign, you should make sure to give them lots of attention when they need it and praise them for getting things done at work or school. Although these people enjoy helping others out, they are also very focused on their goals. To get the most out of them, you should avoid distracting them from their work when they are in the zone. You will be glad that you gave them attention at the end though because they always finish the job quickly and masterfully.

Weaknesses

The weaknesses of the Virgo moon sign include being too critical and lacking a sense of humor sometimes. These people can be challenging to handle when frustrated or upset, so it's best not to upset them in the first place if possible. Also, if you tell one of these people your life story, then don't be surprised if they go into detail about how they would have improved it. They may seem to overanalyze everything. You can expect them to spend more time thinking about what is going on in their lives than actually doing something about it.

People born under this sign love getting involved with lots of different kinds of activities. However, they always feel like there is not enough time for themselves. These people want to get things done right away because they hate putting things off, but unfortunately, this causes them extra stress because they try hard to keep up with everything. To overcome these weaknesses, try to relax and do things at your own pace. You will accomplish more if you are less critical of yourself and others.

It's also important that you learn to laugh sometimes. If anyone knows how to lighten up a situation and find humor in anything, then it's the Virgo moon sign. People born under this sign need people around them to feel like life is worth living. They love being with friends or family just as much as they enjoy helping out in the community! Just remember that they can be very sensitive despite their harsh sense of humor, so it's best not to take them too seriously most of the time.

Libra Moon Sign

The Libra moon sign is ruled by Venus and has an even element of Air. People born under this sign are very indecisive, making it difficult for them to make up their minds about anything. They like having things just the way they are so that they can have a harmonious environment around them. When they aren't working toward perfection, they easily become restless. This need for perfection can cause them to be hard on themselves when things don't go exactly how they planned. The only way that they'll overcome this is if someone encourages them. Being flexible will bring more opportunities to them in the long run. Otherwise, they'll continue on the same self-destructive path until something extreme happens to change their mindsets.

Characteristic Traits

People with a Libra moon sign make great diplomats because they know how to please others. They're always in tune with their surroundings, so they can easily get along with many different kinds of people. On the one hand, this could mean that they'll be able to talk to anyone about anything but, on the other hand, it could also mean that they never say what's really on their minds. This hesitancy is mostly due to fear of rejection or disapproval from others. Their indecisiveness makes it difficult to speak up when something goes wrong or when things need to be fixed.

They're very patient and tolerant in almost all situations. If you try giving them a task or goal with an unknown outcome, you should expect them to take as long as they need to complete it. They're easily bored and have a hard time focusing on one thing at a time, which is why being with other people can be quite difficult for them if they can't find something that interests them. If you want things done now, you'll need to give them some extra incentive or encouragement to get it finished.

Strengths

Libra moon signs are charming and sympathetic, which makes them very likable. They try to do everything peacefully and fairly. They have a propensity for helping others, especially when they can see that there's something wrong with them. Libras believe that all people deserve respect regardless of who they are or what they look like. They are also good mediators because they can sit back and take points from both sides of a situation to create a solution.

They're usually among the first people who try to make peace with others when there's a conflict between two groups. Libras have strong communication skills, which include listening as well as speaking. They like having a harmonious environment around them and can be very helpful if you need them for something.

Weaknesses

This moon sign tends to stray away from goals in favor of pleasure. They believe that everyone is entitled to it, which may cause them to slack off on their work or personal obligations. This attitude leads to procrastination and a lack of self-discipline, as well as poor decision-making in general. They also like being around people who are going through problems because it allows them to fix things, even if they didn't necessarily cause the problem in the first place. If you're a Libra moon sign, you need to work on your discipline. You also need to start accepting responsibility for what you do, even if other people are involved. It will help you a lot in the long run, and it will give you more self-confidence!

Scorpio Moon Sign

People with a Scorpio moon sign are determined, resourceful, and strong-willed. They have an uncanny ability to know what others are hiding from them, making it difficult for them to trust others. This ability is mostly because they're very secretive and private about their own lives. They like being in control of their destiny and don't like being told what to do.

Scorpios are very passionate people who find it difficult to express their emotions verbally. They're very intense in every aspect of their lives, and when they're focused on something, they pay their full attention to it and put all of their energy into it. They prefer things to be a certain way, making them stubborn when defending their opinions. Scorpio moon sign people tend to have a magnetic personality that draws people to them. Even those that aren't overly friendly are very sociable.

Characteristic Traits

Scorpio people are the most complex of all moon signs. They have a great deal of passion, and they express their creativity through intense emotions or physical actions. Scorpio is ruled by Mars, which gives strength to bold actions, determination, courage, and fighting spirits. Those born under this sign are resourceful and have an uncanny ability to uncover secrets.

Scorpios are born investigators. They like knowing the truth and getting to the bottom of things, making them incredibly good at detective work and other professions involving solving cryptic clues. They're very passionate people who experience life on a deep level. While they may not always show it, they have strong feelings about everything that crosses their path.

Strengths

Those born with a Scorpio moon are passionate and intense. They possess incredible strength of character, which makes them capable of going to great lengths to achieve their goals. While they may hide it well, those born under this sign have an incredibly magnetic personality that draws people to them. Although they tend to be private about certain things in life, they're not afraid to get involved in events that affect them.

Scorpios tend to be very good at getting people to open up to them because they possess the ability to tap into people's secrets. Those born under this sign are good at reading people, and they have an impressive ability to uncover mysteries.

People with a Scorpio moon sign tend to be very resourceful, as they can get out of tough situations using their quick thinking and intelligence. They're also quite resourceful at home, as they have a knack for making things with their hands. They're not afraid to take chances in life.

Weaknesses

Scorpio moon sign people tend to be very secretive and private about the personal details of their lives. It's difficult for them to become close friends with others because they don't like being told what to do. Most Scorpios have a deep, dark sense of humor. They like to play pranks on others and enjoy playing practical jokes. The biggest challenge for Scorpio moon sign people is that they often can't stand being around other people with a high opinion of themselves. To overcome these weak points and make the best of their personality, it's helpful for Scorpio moon sign people to surround themselves with other people. It's also helpful to gain the approval of others. These weaknesses can make it very difficult for Scorpio moon sign people to achieve their goals. However, if they can overcome them, they can accomplish almost anything.

This chapter discusses the following four moon signs: Leo, Virgo, Libra, and Scorpio. Leo Moons are passionate people that love to feel appreciated for their efforts. They enjoy being in a leadership position and often volunteer or help out in the community. Virgo Moons like to fix things, and they will give you their full attention when you need them the most. These people possess many strengths that make them excellent choices for jobs: practical nature, sense of responsibility, and ability to work with others. Libra Moons are very social and like to be in a group and be involved in many different activities. They always feel like there is not enough time for themselves. Scorpio Moons are intense, passionate people who enjoy helping others in the community. They are very intuitive.

Chapter 5: Your Moon Signs III

This chapter will cover the third part of moon signs; the Sagittarius, Capricorn, Aquarius, and Pisces Zodiacs. These four zodiacs all have great characteristics that they bring to the world. However, depending on your moon sign, you may not possess these traits immediately. The traits could take a while to develop. There are always good and bad things about every trait of any zodiac. You need to know your traits, but you shouldn't be afraid of them. It is all about learning how to use your traits wisely and positively.

Sagittarius Moon Sign

Sagittarians are energetic and optimistic. They love outdoor activities such as hiking, horseback riding, or any other sport that involves being with nature. Sagittarians tend to be blunt sometimes, but they also speak the truth. This candidness makes people trust them even more because they don't sugarcoat anything. Sagittarians can be hurtful when in an argument, but only because they don't know how to keep their anger in check. They are generally friendly toward everyone around them, and they always seem to have a friend nearby when it's needed the most. They also enjoy good trust and honesty between people. They are never afraid to show their emotions to anyone because it keeps them grounded – and it also means that they are very friendly toward others.

Sagittarians tend not to be as blunt in their conversations, but they can still be straightforward, just like any of the other signs. Their bluntness depends on who they're talking to and what kind of relationship the two share. One major thing about Sagittarius is that many of them want independence from everyone and everything around them but sometimes possess an addictive personality toward certain things. For example, some Sagittarians will obsess over fitness or food, while others will become addicted to less healthy things such as drugs or alcohol. This sort of obsession doesn't mean they are bad people, but it can be challenging to stay on the correct path. It's important to understand that a Sagittarius needs balance in everything that comes into their lives.

Characteristic Traits

Sagittarius is a fire zodiac sign, which means that they are motivated and hardworking. Sagittarius possesses an inquisitive mindset. They are constantly wondering about what's going on in the world around them. However, keeping their minds busy when being curious is not an option. Sagittarians need to keep themselves occupied with other things.

As far as careers go, Sagittarians may be interested in careers that involve travel, such as a flight attendant or something similar. They may also pursue careers that require a lot of thinking and hard work but are still fun. Their minds are always wandering, so Sagittarians have very high expectations of themselves and others around them.

In relationships, they tend to focus on their independence more than anything else. However, this doesn't mean they don't want a relationship because it's the opposite! If they get into a committed relationship with someone and have more than just physical attraction, it means the person has earned their trust completely. They will forever be there whenever needed, even if neither of them shares the same feelings at that moment in time.

Strengths

Sagittarians will possess abilities that can take them far in life. They are intelligent and extremely hardworking. They won't let anything hold them back from reaching their goals, and they are willing to work as hard as they need to if something is worth it. A Sagittarius also has a personality that allows them to trust others very easily. This means you should be able to trust every Sagittarius you meet because they will never betray your trust in any kind of way.

The energy level possessed by a Sagittarius is very high, making this zodiac sign extraverted. They are always looking to socialize with more people, and they don't care what the situation is. They can make friends in almost any kind of environment, whether it's a party or any other kind of social gathering. Sagittarians also have minds that allow them to be curious all the time, and they will learn something new every day without trying too hard.

Weaknesses

A Sagittarius definitely has weaknesses. They tend to develop addictions to things like food or drugs but try to hide this from others while secretly pursuing them. To avoid these problems, a Sagittarius should make sure to maintain a healthy relationship with everyone around them so there won't ever be any mistrust or unwanted problems.

Advice: Try to stay as positive as possible. Remember that patience is a virtue and will help you greatly! Understand the difference between friendliness and rudeness. Don't let your bluntness hurt anyone's feelings because everyone makes mistakes. So don't make the mistake of being too harsh on them. Be calm and rational during arguments or when you are expressing your emotions. Find peace in everything around you by staying as balanced as you can! Share your thoughts more often about certain topics, so you get to know others better without being rude or offensive!

Capricorn Moon Sign

It's a cardinal sign, which means that Capricorns are motivated and hardworking. They will also have a curious mindset. Capricorn tends to be very ambitious in whatever they do, even if it just involves relaxing. They pay attention to everything because of how curious they can get about things that don't matter to others. They think highly of themselves and what they've done in life so far.

In relationships, they tend to focus on individuality more than anything else. However, they are also very loyal to the people that they are with. They tend to keep their feelings hidden from those they care about, but once you get them out of that shell, you can have a long and happy relationship with them.

Capricorns have great leadership qualities and can take charge if need be, even if they aren't in any sort of position to control anyone else. They may become leaders by taking charge of themselves or others depending on the situation. They may even become followers if they see someone else is better equipped to lead.

Characteristic Traits

Capricorns are generally strong and ambitious. They tend to be hard workers, but they also have a higher chance of developing stress in their life. Stress isn't always bad, though, because Capricorns seem to work better under pressure, leading to success in the end if they let themselves get stressed over certain situations in their life.

They like to take care of things, and they normally do things that need immediate attention right away. Sometimes this can hold them back from doing other things with their free time because they are so used to taking care of important things first instead of putting them off or never dealing with them.

They are also very independent people. They usually do their own thing and get on with what they want to do without letting anyone else influence them or their decisions. If someone tried to stop them while working toward something, it could cause a small uproar between the Capricorn and that person because of how much pride they have in themselves and how much they want to accomplish that others couldn't do before them.

Strengths

Capricorns are generally great with money. They are also very ambitious and hardworking, which may help them in their lives by giving them the motivation needed to do whatever they set their minds to and accomplish everything they need on time. These types of characteristics are great for work and school.

Capricorns have a sense of humor, but it is usually dark or sarcastic. They don't always use their sense of humor, but when they do, you will realize that Capricorns have more life experience than it might seem. They also have a good sense of what will happen in the future, but they may be too focused on the goals so that they could miss out on opportunities that could have made them more successful had they noticed them earlier.

Weaknesses

Capricorns tend to stress themselves out a lot over how long things take to accomplish, making them lose focus on what they need to get done and become distracted by something else due to their abundant curiosity. They also tend to not share with those around them because of their independence, which leads to others misunderstanding them and even hating them simply because they do not know the true person behind the mask.

Advice: Don't hold grudges against anyone. If you do, you'll never find happiness in a relationship or with yourself. Learn from your mistakes and try not to make the same ones again. And if you can't seem to get over someone, learn to live without them so that you don't ruin your future by focusing on something that happened in the past.

Aquarius Moon Sign

Those born with the Aquarius moon sign are usually described by their family and friends as independent, rebellious, original, unique, creative, compromising to a certain extent but mostly single-minded. They like to find new experiences and surroundings since they love variety. Their world is subjective of their moods which can be erratic at times. They may prefer some emotional distance between themselves and the rest of the world. However, all these traits make up an interesting character that never fails to fascinate those around them.

The tendency of this moon sign is toward humanism in all things from philosophy to art to politics. This sign loves change for change's sake, so they sometimes cause upheavals without thinking about the consequences.

Aquarius moon signs are idealistic, but they can be cold and inflexible. There is a tendency to be aloof in their dealings with others, as they tend not to reveal their inner thoughts and feelings easily. They have an easy time with people who share the same life perspective and approach, but otherwise, they may lead a lonely life. They may also isolate themselves from the world, feeling that everything and everyone is against them. However, if given enough attention and love, these individuals make good friends with those who know how to handle them.

Characteristic Traits

The sign Aquarius is ruled by Uranus, which gives us the typical traits of an Aquarian personality. The qualities that you display the most are originality and rebelliousness. You have a strong sense of individuality even if you belong to a group. You may be somewhat unemotional while engaging with people, but you make up for it with your witty comments and sarcastic remarks amongst close friends or family members. You can be quite detached from other people's emotions but sensitive to their needs. However, due to this characteristic, you may appear cold toward some people, and they may feel that they are not important enough for you to invest time in them.

Strengths

Aquarians can be objective and detached from their own emotions. This gives them a lot of strength, especially in life-threatening situations, as they can make decisions without having any emotional baggage associated with it. These individuals also have a strong sense of individuality and the need for freedom, allowing them to break away from powerful norms even if doing so ruffles some feathers. Due to this nature, they can easily climb up the corporate ladder or become successful entrepreneurs.

Weaknesses

The Aquarian moon zodiac sign has many weaknesses due to being emotionally detached from other people or things around them. Since these people decide everything by themselves, they may not get what they want at times because others disagree with their ideas. They can also be judgmental toward others which makes them appear cold and unemotional. People with an Aquarius moon sign are also known for being so tactless in most situations that they would never think about the implications of their actions first before actually doing them.

The Fixed Air element associated with this sign can keep an Aquarius calm under pressure. Still, suppose there is a lot of emotional baggage attached to the situation. In that case, these individuals will feel disconcerted and may react irrationally or aggressively because of their inability to control their emotions.

Advice: You should try to avoid any sudden changes or movements in your life because this may have repercussions on your emotional well-being and will also trigger impulsive actions. The best way for you to handle these situations is by thinking through them before actually doing anything else, as it would help you remain calm under pressure. You need to break away from the herd and do what's right for you. Otherwise, you are too much of a conformist at heart, but you enjoy life so much more when you go against conventions once in a while *just for the sake of doing so.*

Pisces Moon Sign

Pisces is the twelfth and last sign of the zodiac, and it can be difficult to find an accurate description of how these individuals behave. Pisceans are known as dreamy and imaginative people who ignore practicalities in favor of helping others or just lazily floating through life. However, what most people don't know about this sign is that every Pisces hides a very determined and hardworking personality, doing whatever they want without being told to do so.

Characteristic Traits

A water element governs the sign Pisces, and that makes them detached from reality at times. These individuals tend to enjoy the company of other people but may appear aloof or emotionally detached. They also have a strong sense of imagination, allowing them to see things in a subjective way rather than from an objective viewpoint. Pisces moon sign individuals are quite sensitive and caring toward others without getting too emotionally attached.

Strengths

Despite their relaxed nature, you can rely on Pisceans when it comes to taking care of themselves because they would always do whatever it takes to ensure that they're physically healthy before anything else. That applies to the people around them as well. This quality makes them so charming as companions since they will never let you down – even if they cannot spend much time with you. Since they care for your physical well-being, you can trust them with your personal matters as well.

Weaknesses

Pisces Moon sign individuals are known for their egotism and overindulgence in fantasies which eventually drains them of all energy, leaving them vulnerable to any emotional triggers and prone to breakdowns. Their sensitivity also makes it difficult for them to maintain relationships since they tend to see things from an unrealistic point of view. Pisceans often let their emotions dictate their actions rather than being guided by logic and reason. This may lead to irrational behavior on your part, especially when you become too attached to someone or something, which could lead you to do reckless things.

Advice: Pisces need to eliminate the habit of ignoring practicality so that they can do whatever they think is right. It may end up being so wrong that you'll regret not listening to the advice of the people close to you. Pisceans need to grow up and take responsibility for their actions rather than run away from them or just ignore them altogether. You should learn how to live your own life by accepting a certain amount of risk so that you won't be bogged down by regret at a later time.

This chapter has given you a brief introduction to the zodiac signs of Sagittarius, Capricorn, Aquarius, and Pisces. Sagittarians are active, adventurous, and love to travel. They have a great sense of humor with an optimistic outlook on life. Capricorns like being in charge, so they work hard for the things they want in life. Aquarians bring balance because their main goal is peace of mind. Pisces are sensitive, intuitive, and emotional creatures who need lots of attention from others!

Chapter 6: The Lunar South Node: Your Past Life

If you've been into Astrology for a while now, you probably already know that since the moment you were born, the stars in the sky are aligned in a certain way that reflects your life's purpose. Your personal birth or natal chart is mapped out from the first breath you take. Many believers in Astrology use this unique configuration to provide a lifetime of learning. Birth charts and South Node signs can help you unlock several possibilities, identify your potential growth, and provide you with clues as to your destiny or purpose. They also help draw attention to the areas in our lives where we cling to our habits too much. According to Astrology, these habits (the ones we do automatically without even thinking about them) are considered Karma or South Node habits. In this chapter, we take a closer look at the South Node signs of the moon and how these particular positions affect your Karma and past life.

What Is the Lunar South Node in Astrology?

Each person possesses special traits that have been embedded within their personality from the moment they were born. We are all born with inner weaknesses and strengths that we hold on to, whether we do it consciously or subconsciously. In Astrology, these qualities are believed to follow us from our past lives, and they eventually become part of us. Your South Node signs represent the people you were before you came into this current life. However, the qualities associated with these signs are the ones you're meant to leave behind to achieve personal fulfillment. We are all meant to become someone different in this life, even if we are used to certain habits that are difficult to let go of.

Your birth chart includes two important aspects, the South and North nodes, which are connected even though they're opposite nodes that drive opposite behaviors and personality traits. These nodes are not planets. They are two opposing intersection points made up of the moon's orbit and the ecliptic plane on your birth date. Both points are referred to as lunar nodes. The South node describes the person or qualities you should leave behind, while the North node represents the person you should try to become and the qualities you should work on gaining. Without working on dropping your negative traits, you may never feel fulfilled or achieve personal growth in your life.

The South Node in Each Sign

The entire Astrology culture is built on the belief in reincarnation and Karma. According to Astrology, our past lives are supposed to help us become better equipped for the challenges of each life we live. Your South node sign is different from your main astrological sign. Instead, it represents the qualities of the sign that you should try to avoid. We continue to come back as bodies on Earth, and as long as that keeps happening, we will always face new challenges. Let's get into more detail about what each sign represents as a South node and how you should work on yourself to come closer to the qualities of your North node.

The South Node in Aries

If your South node in Aries indicates that you lacked perspective and were selfish about your needs in your past life, you have always loved to be the center of attention and have subconsciously overlooked other people's needs. It has always felt natural to you to act ruthlessly. Aggression is your default coping mechanism. However, you're also unstoppable when it comes to getting what you really want. What you need to do in this life is to overcome your increased passion, commit to your partnerships, and cooperate more with others. You should work on achieving more inner peace rather than chasing the dream of being the best. Aries tend to be impulsive, and they rush into quick decisions, which is something you need to work on! Sometimes, you may need to listen more and acknowledge that other people may have different points of view.

The South Node in Taurus

Taurus South node indicates a past materialistic life. You've been surrounded by everything you want, from security to luxurious earthly treasures that helped you survive for too long. This fortunate standing in life gives you many materialistic traits. You seek wealth and other tangible treasures. You may also naturally feel that you're responsible for everyone around you. Well, it's time to let go. It's not your responsibility to take care of those around you to the point of ignoring your mental health. It's also time to start searching for spiritual gratification (and overcome your fear of the unknown). Instead of chasing earthly leisure, you should be looking for a deeper journey. Focus on your spiritual instincts and let them guide you instead of depending on the practicality of your earthly possessions. It's all about embracing the non-material side of your personality.

The South Node in Gemini

You've lived a dishonest past life, and you could always get yourself out of the toughest situations with your words. You always refuse to be held accountable for any situation, even if you caused it. In this life, you should focus on speaking more truthfully instead of engaging in time-wasting drama. Focus on being more productive and stay away from your two-faced nature that influences your decisions. Only make room for one personality to take over and use it to increase your productivity. You should also be taking more risks and looking at the world differently. It's not as dark a place as you think, so get out there, travel, and see the world. You can miss many opportunities by staying in your comfort zone, so the goal is to be more productive and take more risks.

The South Node in Cancer

You have a codependent personality that prioritizes the needs of other people around you over your personal needs. You're too focused on receiving affection from those around you, and you lack self-reliance. However, it's time for you to be more comfortable staying alone. Stop letting your fear of being left alone keep you from going after your dreams. It's also time to stop seeking affection from others and to focus on yourself at all times. Start listening to your head more, in the same way you'd let your heart have a say in every decision. Sometimes, it's okay to be selfish and put your own needs first, so stop wasting your energy on people around you and engage in more self-care activities. Your purpose is to love yourself and shift your attention to self-development to feel fulfilled in this life.

The South Node in Leo

You've suffered in the past when no one was there to see your sacrifices. So, now it's time to focus on moving on rather than taking things personally all the time. You should understand that everyone else around you has their problems, and nobody has time to deal with your conflicts. You tend to overestimate your power all the time, but it's time to let go of the past and become more down-to-earth. You should also overcome your obsession with attention and vanity, instead, show affection to those around you and pay more attention to their needs. Don't let your past define you, and be more open to change. It's not always necessary to be in the spotlight or be the best at what you do. The more open-minded you become, the fewer problems you will have in your relationships.

The South Node in Virgo

The past lives of a South node Virgo lacked mystery and were obsessed with control. You tend to overanalyze everything around you, even the beautiful things, until they start to look ugly. You investigate even the smallest details and continue to look for a straightforward answer. In this life, you need to embrace other forms of healing and art, such as using your imagination and writing poetry. You don't have to be in control all the time. It's only making you anxious, so let go. You can find peace and serenity in mystery. You can pursue something deeper in life if you switch your attention from yourself. That's all a Virgo needs to mature and to let go of their past lives.

The South Node in Libra

You have a long past of letting your friends steal your thunder, and you tend to give up the spotlight so that you can avoid conflict. This time you should go after your dreams and let your name be known. You always ignore your personal needs to achieve peace, but you need to be more selfish and draw attention to your opinions. Even if it causes controversy or leads to conflict, the most important thing is to speak up and let your opinions be known. You can't survive in the shadow of others, and maintaining your relationships is not more important than your comfort. While most Librans try to avoid it, a conflict is not the worst thing in the world. So be more courageous in expressing yourself and make your opinions known.

The South Node in Scorpio

You need to stop being so possessive and manipulative all the time. Your past life's power was to use temptation to get others to do what you wanted. You're also so reliant on their kindness that it's hard for you to let go and provide for yourself. You need to leave those qualities behind in this life and start depending more upon yourself for emotional support. Build your foundation and create your own ways as others will follow when you focus on yourself and achieve success. Unlike many other South node signs, a Scorpio must focus on tangible things rather than getting too caught up in what they can't control. You can't control everything and everyone, so shift your attention to what you *can* change.

The South Node in Sagittarius

Sagittarius South nodes express their philosophies loudly and base their problem-solving decisions on unrealistic and fanciful ideas. However, they always seem to lack focus on the matter at hand. To feel more fulfilled in this life, you need to ground yourself or settle somewhere. You need to give yourself time to focus fully on the objective truth instead of chasing esoteric theories or ideas. Understand that the adventures you engage in are only a coping mechanism to avoid certain areas in your life. Most of the time, you're running away from yourself, trying to find an escape from people who are distant from you or places that are far away. Unfortunately, this comes with great sacrifices, and you'll eventually lose it if you don't pay attention to what you have. Get closer to your roots, stop taking or indulging, and start exchanging equally with other people around you.

The South Node in Capricorn

Your past life has taught you that success and wealth bring happiness and inner peace. Now, these two qualities have burned you out so much that you're left alone with an empty heart. You're isolated, and the only thing you know by nature is overworking yourself. However, it can be a toxic trait sometimes if you start believing that you're superior to others. You also mute your intuition and neglect the relationships in your life, but it's time to change that. Listen more to your intuition and value your partnerships and relationships. Sometimes, you need to realize that the people you love are more important than your success. Make that clear and express your affection. Surrounding yourself with your wealth is only going to push people away. Always choose love over materialism.

The South Node in Aquarius

Aquarius South nodes are known to be relaxed but supportive when you need them. This is only at their own expense. If your South node sign is Aquarius, you need to stop hiding your feelings. You think that showing emotions will make you look weak or alienate your peers, but this is not true. Even if it's true, who cares? Understand that your emotions matter and that you need to listen to your heart more often. Avoiding the discomfort of others will only cause you to bottle up your feelings and overlook things that really matter to you. Your needs are more important than the satisfaction of your community, so make sure you express them clearly. You've already been taking care of everyone's feelings for too long. In this life, it's all about listening to your true self and getting you what you need.

The South Node in Pisces

If your South Node is Pisces, it indicates that you may have been a passive person who watched their life go downhill without really doing anything about it. You keep thinking that there's nothing that can help you take control of your fate. Focus on reality. Stand up for your opinions, and don't let others abuse or use you like you always do. Stop playing the role of the victim and start taking action when it comes to the problems in your life. Your goal is to become more concerned with objectivity and look away from your irrational theories and thoughts.

Deciphering the Karmic Signature

If we let our karma or South Node qualities take over, we will lead a life of stagnation and never find our true purpose for this life. This is why it's important to understand our karmic signature, which refers to the meaning behind our South Node signs. Many books and articles mention numerous techniques that we can apply to understand the cosmic position of our South Nodes and how this affects our karma. Some of the most dominant studies illustrated a very helpful technique using Pablo Picasso's Gemini South Node.

Picasso's South Node is located at 10 degrees of the Curiosity sign, Gemini, which lies in the 11th house of groups according to the birth chart of lunar nodes. According to the chart, his rebellion was classified in the 5th house of love affairs, shown in his countless number of women and partners. His karma was falling for peer pressure and trying to belong. Let's use Picasso's birth chart to get into more detail about interpreting the karmic signature.

Assess the Qualities of the Planet that Rules the South Node Sign

The science of Astrology and planets is very interesting to people who are into human psychology. It's compelling to read about how the planets that express each sign represent a spectrum of human behavior and personality types. For example, in Picasso's case, the ruler planet of his south node sign is Mercury, representing curious types of people. Some other signs may have more than one planetary ruler. For example, Aquarius has Saturn, the Hermit type, and Uranus, the Rebel type.

Identify the House Position of the South Node and Establish the Biographical Content

This part of the analysis is where we acknowledge our long-term goals and make connections to get closer to them. In Picasso's example, and as previously mentioned, his SN is located in the 11th house of groups. Here, Picasso's karma was the inability to break the restrictions of the group and their judgments toward him. In other examples, the South Node can be located in the house of pleasure or fun. This type's karma can be related to the inability to entertain oneself or find joy in individuality.

Look for Ways to Attain the Goals of the South Node Sign

There is always a goal for each Astrological sign. These signs represent your values and priorities. They always guide you to a certain extent, which is believed to be supported by the movement of planets. If we take Picasso's example, his South Node was in the Gemini region. This type thrives on new information and uses a young person's curiosity to get what they want. They always seem edgy and bubbly, but their goal is to focus on themselves and become more productive. Read more into the goals of your SN sign and figure out if they align with your life purposes.

Connect the South Node Ruler with Its Position

Even though Gemini SNs are curious, the group hinders their desire to search or understand everything around them. The ruler of Picasso's SN was Mercury which lies in the 4th house family, implying a tendency to follow external influences. Now, both houses on the chart, the SN's house, and the ruling planet's house, suggest that Picasso's personality was highly overwhelmed by the crowd.

Look into the Planetary Ruler's Sign

On the birth chart of lunar nodes, you can determine the signs of the planet that rules your South Node sign. This lets you tap into even more knowledge around how your type behaves and perceives life. Picasso's ruler planet, Mercury, was in the Scorpio sign area, and this translates to the type that always stretches into unprecedented new models. It shows a fascination or obsession with taboos.

Put Everything Together

If we look at Picasso's lunar positions and house groups, we can see many contradictions between them. However, the point is to determine your life purpose and understand your karma before it has a chance to take over your destiny. Gather all the information you come up with after studying your birth chart and SN, and ask yourself whether there is anything else left unresolved. Is there a dream or person you're longing for that was never there before? Assess your SN qualities and be open to getting closer to your North Node qualities to feel more fulfilled in life.

Our lunar South and North nodes determine a lot about how we are supposed to live our lives. These signs always hint at something. They guide you to your true fate and help you overcome the qualities of your past lives – an important reason to learn about all your South node classifications. Focus on approaching your North node goals and qualities to become better equipped to deal with the upcoming challenges.

Chapter 7: The Lunar North Node: Your Life Purpose

The North Node shows us the things and experiences we must go through to develop and grow spiritually. We are unique human beings with our unique paths in life, and our North Node helps clarify the path.

The North Node shows us where we can grow or expand and gives us the ability to integrate important life lessons. It may feel good or stifling to think that your North Node clarifies your purpose or destiny. Perhaps you don't want to feel like destiny is in place, and you would prefer to choose your own. But your North Node is not forcing you along any particular path. Instead, it shows you where you would feel the most fulfilled and aligned. Each of us has a destiny or purpose in this life, and being aware of your North Node and your unique purpose makes things just a little easier for you.

What Is the Lunar North Node in Astrology?

When reading about your North Node, you may not resonate with it. However, this does not mean it is inaccurate. Your North Node merely shows you where you can expand, evolve, and grow. It does not mean this is how you are already. It just points to your innate skills and characteristics. Due to conditioning and life events, many of us lose touch with our inner selves. We feel like strangers to ourselves, and our authentic nature is pushed down.

Learning about your North Node may feel a little bit like learning about a stranger, but it illustrates to you what your soul needs. Don't be afraid to leave your comfort zone, and let these new qualities and attitudes take form in your life. It may feel awkward or unnatural at first, but give it some time. Try it on for size, and see how you can slowly begin to adjust your approach and thoughts to align with your North Node.

Your North Node is essentially your roadmap to success, and it certainly won't look like anyone else's or resemble the standard view of success. Permit yourself to shed these societal standards to give yourself the highest chance in life.

The North Node in Each Sign

As explained in the previous chapter, the whole Astrology belief system is built upon Karma and how humans go through their many lives. We are reincarnated in different forms of lives each time, and our South node represents our karma or the qualities we should try to avoid. Oppositely, your North Node is the sign you should try to become closer to, and therefore, you'll have a fixed opposite North node to your South one. Let's take a look at how this looks and what the North node represents in each sign.

Aries

When the North Node is in Aries, the south is in libra. Remember, the North and South Nodes, just like the directions, are directly opposite each other. Together they form the nodal axis. If you know what one node is, you will automatically know the other.

If your North Node is in Aries, you might find that you would do best to balance looking after yourself with looking after others. You should be focused on yourself by healing, evolving, and growing in a way that allows you to flourish. Move away from feelings and attitudes of dependency on others. You could easily form codependent patterns with others. Instead, learn to detach. Begin to do things for yourself, learn who you really are and what you truly want.

The more authentic you become, the more fulfilled you will feel. Ignore the things that lead you toward attachment, external opinions, thoughts, and feelings. Go inwards and seek internal validation. It will help you develop the independence you need to walk the path of your destiny more easily.

Your life should revolve around bringing your passionate ideas to fruition. You are a warrior in your lifetime, so stay on this path. You will often find yourself being a pioneer on a path toward love and justice.

Learn to live alone, to be by yourself, for yourself.

Taurus

With your North Node in Taurus, it is important to let go of the needs of others. Discover yourself, and begin to develop self-reliance. You must start to establish deep self-worth within yourself. Nothing and no one outside of you can provide you with that. The more you look for it anywhere else, you move further away from your path.

To walk the path of purpose, you need to be able to give yourself what you need without relying on others.

Your sign appreciates beauty, pleasure, and love. You need to learn what you truly value, as this will help you manifest the beautiful things you want in your life. Don't self-sabotage by feeling unworthy. Instead, know that you are truly worth everything you desire and more. Allow yourself to receive from the goodness of the universe.

Gemini

The Gemini North Node is on this planet to connect to others. You can relate and communicate with others easily. The wisdom that you have stored inside of you is ready to be shared. You love to share information and exchange ideas and knowledge. Use this to help you determine where your natural talents lie.

You may feel the urge to share with others through writing, speaking, reporting, teaching, marketing, or even just having a conversation. You may become a writer, a poet, a teacher, or someone that strikes up conversation wherever you go. This ability to communicate and share ideas will help you walk the path of your destiny, giving you clarity and fulfillment.

You will often find that you can sit with others and discuss opposing ideas without feeling the need to force your ideas. You can easily see both sides of the coin and weigh up either side, giving you the ability to learn and share knowledge, ideas, and wisdom objectively. You are not always swayed by emotions or unconscious bias, and this will help you make decisions rationally and objectively.

Cancer

The Cancer North Node might feel like they struggle to balance their family and career. Part of your life purpose is to build a healthy family experience and home. These mean a lot to you and add to your feelings of happiness and stability.

You need to create a nurturing and safe space for yourself and your family, helping you along your path. It is okay to be vulnerable, to let go of rigidity and expectations. Perfection should be left behind so you can truly step into your authentic and aligned self.

It may be hard for you to achieve your desires when you are holding so tightly onto them. Instead, let go a little, and witness how much easier it is. It's okay to let go of seriousness, and you may find that your life falls into a natural flow.

Leo

The Leo North Node is very likely to be comfortable being the extroverted, open, and social fire sign. You may be affectionate and incredibly vibrant and bold. The spotlight was made for you, so don't be afraid to step into it when you need to. When someone opens up the space for you to take a central role, take it as your right.

Get used to making big moves without fear, opening up entirely new paths for you. Your open and affectionate nature invites people in and makes you someone that can easily relate to others. You can make tons of new friends and create a large network thanks to your natural ability to be vibrant and inviting. Use this to help you walk your life path.

Know that you are always being invited to take up space. It is your birthright, and you are here to express yourself. Step into the magic of who you are, and continue to make choices that leave you feeling empowered. The more empowered and creative you feel, the closer you become to your destiny.

Virgo

The North Node Virgo may find a lot of satisfaction from being practical and detail orientated. Your life may become a little easier by developing a healthy routine and a set of rules around your daily life. This doesn't mean you turn into a type A, but establishing rules and routines will help you significantly.

Setting clear and defined goals helps you achieve your destiny. The clarity and purpose of your life will manifest when you set out to achieve it in a practical and organized manner. Of course, you shouldn't abandon all emotions or feelings. Instead, your intuition should be finely balanced with logic and intellect in every part of your life, helping you make the right choices.

Setting boundaries with both yourself and others is important. You become empowered through being focused and organized. Acting in this way gives you the confidence and energy you need to achieve your goals.

The North Node Virgo is a healer. Part of your destiny on this planet is to heal. You may find yourself serving others and being devoted to healing. You are here to find the meaning of unconditional love.

Libra

The North Node Libra should focus on being kind and just – the attitude with which you face life. Competition should be avoided, and instead, you should dedicate yourself to forming meaningful bonds with others. It is important that you are sensitive to others and what they feel and desire.

You are on this planet to learn about relationships, commitments, and partnerships. If you find yourself with a past littered with relationship or commitment issues, this allows you to learn the lessons necessary to evolve into who you are meant to be. Don't view these experiences negatively but, instead, view them for what they truly are, a lesson to learn to reach your true self.

You are here to learn how to have a relationship with someone without developing codependency or abandoning yourself. You must find the balance between yourself and others.

You have innate leadership skills and often pride yourself on your independence. It would be best if you learned to become diplomatic when you communicate. Libra is associated with justice, and with your North Node Libra, this may indicate being on a path to create justice for yourself or others.

Scorpio

The Scorpio North Node is here to bring forward the energies of passion and freedom. In this lifetime, you are here to release attachments and feel truly free. You must work through any attachment issues and deal with any fears related to feeling controlled. The two may appear hand in hand in some circumstances, and this only occurs for you to achieve transcendence even faster.

Your soul has this deep desire to change, evolve, and grow. Listen to this call, and don't allow yourself to get sucked in by other people and eternal attachments. Your life is a journey of continuous release that will lead you to your most authentic self.

It would help if you learned to deal with life fearlessly, and any crisis or sudden change that occurs should be dealt with head-on. You must get comfortable with transforming and shedding old identities and beliefs. This opens you up to beautiful mystical experiences.

Sagittarius

The Sagittarius North Node is here to escape their comfort zone. You need to get away from home and seek out expansive experiences all around the world. The wisdom you need may lie in any corner of the Earth. You are here to live a big life, inspiring others with your actions and vision. Freedom is often your main priority, so allow it to guide you.

The vision you have and the actions you take to achieve it inspire those around you. You are here to make big moves, so fight any fear. Perhaps previous conditioning or other aspects of your life hold you back from living your life in an intended way. Know that you are here to truly inspire others, and the more aligned you become, the easier it is for you to do that.

Don't rely too much on logic, and instead, use your intuition to guide you, as this will help you make the best decisions and choices. Choosing to be more logical and rational may mean coming across big, exciting opportunities. Tune into your intuition to master your reality and bring forward the experiences that help you along on your journey to your destiny.

Capricorn

The Capricorn North Node is here to help you develop into a strong and independent character. You need to take radical responsibility for your actions to take complete control of your life. The more accountability you take, the more aligned you become.

Realize life is not happening to you. Instead, it is happening for you. The things that occur around you are happening because of you. You must be able to adjust your behavior, energy, attitudes, and thoughts so that you can manifest the things you truly want.

If you don't assume a certain level of accountability, you may find that the things that manifest into your life are happening based on negative beliefs that you chose to ignore. Be brave enough to face the mistakes and habits that keep you from blossoming into your true self.

Alongside this sense of responsibility, balance it out with sensitivity. You are a leader, and you can achieve great things. Capricorn is a hardworking sign, and you are here to own these leadership abilities and show others how to make great strides just as you have. Own this part of you and shed any shame surrounding these leadership desires. This is your destiny and your birthright.

To reach the emotional and financial status you want, define your goals practically and maturely. Let go of any external attachments to see your goals and desires come to fruition. Attachments may hold you back from prospering into the person you have the potential to become.

Aquarius

The Aquarius North Node is here to help you to be carefree and liberated. It would help if you had time to be alone, savor solitude, and rid yourself of the desire to need validation from others. You may even find yourself being validated, but the things you want are often only a distraction, so detach yourself from these feelings and go inwards. This is where you will find greater fulfillment.

You are here to be innovative and authentic to yourself. You can aid in creating a world where others can also step into their own authenticity. The innovative aspects of this placement help you make the world better and freer for others.

In relationships, you must shed fears for your partner to be themselves instead of what you want them to be. Every person is equal and has the right to be treated in a just manner. Use this to help direct your relationships with others.

The Aquarius North Nodes are humanitarians, and the more you focus on making a difference, the more fulfilled you will feel. Embrace your eccentric attitudes and unique self, as doing this wholeheartedly will help give others the confidence and power to do the same.

You will find that you thrive in a community and when working with a team, although you should always ensure you remain calm, collected, and able to consider other people in any situation. Allow your humanitarian instincts to guide you as you chase your goals.

Pisces

The Pisces North Nodes are here to move with the flow of life and to let go of any tight grip on routine or rules. You should heal feelings of guilt and trust that there is a larger plan in place. The more you allow yourself to relax with the flow of life, the more aligned you will become with your destiny. Allow yourself to relax, and you will see that the doors of destiny open up with ease.

Your intuition is important, and you should begin to develop sensitivities to be in touch with it. It is intuition that will help guide you to make the right choices and decisions.

Self-love is key here, and developing this allows you to trust the greater plan in place. It will help you make choices from a place of ease and fulfillment. This self-love also helps you treat others with compassion and respect.

It may be odd when you don't feel like your North Node accurately represents you. This is normal because your North Node is more of a map to your success. Allow yourself to feel the gap between who you are now and who you can be, and use it to give you the boost to make the necessary changes.

You don't need to change all at once. Begin slowly, and start to add one new attitude or line of thinking to your life. Try it on for size, and see how it feels to be that person. If it feels too odd, take it down a notch until it feels more comfortable, and then slowly increase the feeling until you naturally become that individual.

This process should be one of enjoyment, so allow yourself to know that it is always for your own good. It does not always have to be a struggle but instead, choose to adjust and add these changes to your life slowly. You might resonate with some aspects of your North Node, but not with all the others.

The North Node is a roadmap to your success, but the road map is littered with lessons – which is how you come into your success. The quicker you can transcend your circumstances and issues, the quicker you achieve success. Dive deep into your North Node and witness the transformation ahead of you.

Chapter 8: The Moon with Other Planets

The relationship of the Moon with other planets is quite intricate. Ancient Vedic astrologers deemed the Moon to be the queen or ruler of the nine imperial planets. As the lunar cycle passes and enters a new phase every 2 to 3 days, it also shifts its position in relevance to other planets. While the Moon develops a strong relationship with some planets, it simply touches the roots of other celestial bodies. This chapter covers the Moon's distinct effects as a sole body and in conjunction with each planet. Along with this, we will also draw parallels between the Moon's behavior during the conjunction in the natal chart and the transit phase.

The Conjunction of the Moon with Other Planets

When the Moon is entering a different phase and shifts its position, it is known to be in "transit." It can affect its conjunction with other planets and manipulate their qualities too. As the name suggests, the Moon in transit is constantly shifting or moving. When we talk about the correlation of transits in natal charts, we are actually looking at the Moon's position and movement in relevance to a specific planet at a given moment. The natal and transit elements of natives can heavily influence their characteristics and personality.

Moon and Mercury

Mercury symbolizes the nervous system and the mind. When the planet affiliates with the Moon, representing the soul and mind, the conjunction results in an adaptable and wise disposition. Collectively, the celestial bodies influence an emotionally stable and conscious environment. People with this conjunction on their natal charts can express their emotions and feelings with ease. Their ability to express their feelings with ease also helps them make honest friends. This conjunct in the Transit phase can result in heightened sensitivity and emotional vulnerability. The native can also experience more mood swings now and then.

Born under the Moon-Mercury conjunction, you will likely be blessed with creativity, wisdom, and oratory skills. However, the native often lacks the ability to focus, resulting in poor decision-making skills, leading to instability in their personal and professional lives. Despite lacking mindfulness skills, the native can still fulfill difficult tasks due to their sharp mind. They need to boost their concentration levels and sharpen their attention. Failing to do so can lead to negative repercussions and the development of vices like alcohol abuse, addiction to gambling, or cheating. In some cases, the person can also develop such habits due to being pushed into a downward spiral, affecting their personal life and career.

If they fail to pull themselves up, they will likely become cheats, criminals, or fraudsters. Their charming personality may fool others into believing them. Even if they have bad intentions, others may refuse to believe it due to their attractive demeanor. If the conjunction affiliates with atrocious malefic, the person can turn into a nasty criminal.

Moon and Venus

Venus represents air and symbolizes feminine energy – just like the Moon – creating a kind, gentle, and loving personality, which helps the native form strong relationships. Everyone gets along with the native when the conjunct occurs in the natal chart. The person possesses great imagination powers and can maintain harmonious personal and professional relationships. Due to this, they also have a huge network and a healthy social life. Since they are quite outgoing and extroverted by nature, the natives are often concerned about their looks and pay extra attention to grooming. They focus on their style and hardly step out without getting ready.

Due to their emotional availability, the person can have a happy and loving family. They are loyal to their spouse and deeply care about their children. They have a keen eye for art and a love of gathering exotic objects. Individuals with a well-balanced Moon-Venus conjunction are known to be talented gardeners and indulge in landscaping. They also love animals and are often found adopting pets. Their love and care for their loved ones are reciprocated, inspiring the native to build more lasting bonds.

This affiliation can bring issues in the individual's married life if they get overly sensitive during the transit state. In general, they are more relaxed in this state and prefer to hang out with their loved ones. Since the person is likely to be more popular in their social group, they also attract sexual relationships and energy. When buying artistic or designer objects, they value their worth and do not mind spending more money on valuable items. They believe in self-care routines and often pamper themselves by shopping, visiting spas, or getting a haircut.

Moon and Rahu

The Moon needs to be in the waxing or complete phase during the conjunction with Rahu to get better results. If it is in the waning phase, it can become weaker during transit. The native possesses exemplary imaginative powers, which can also lead to increased sensitivity and the development of psychic abilities. In extreme cases, they will likely start overthinking and get influenced by their surroundings. They will seek validation from others and fall victim to unhealthy environments and toxicity. The natives can also attract toxic people if they become vulnerable. To avoid this, they should choose their environment and friends with care and precision. If you fail to monitor Rahu, it can turn monstrous and push you into a deep well of desires. Over time, the demonic energy will also instigate you into copying others.

This conjunction can be dangerous and results in the development of mental health illnesses like obsessive-compulsive disorder or depression. Typically, children are easily influenced by this conjunction. If parents fail to monitor their behavior, they may develop vices and bad habits. Over time, it can be difficult to pull them out. It is necessary to bring positive influences into their lives to keep Rahu from overshadowing the Moon's power. Whether it's your natal chart or the transit phase, Rahu's dominance can majorly impact your life. Keep away from overindulgence and enjoy things in moderation.

Moon and Ketu

While this conjunction is majorly perceived as a negative affiliation, certain aspects favor the combination of Moon and Ketu. In general, Ketu possesses feminine energy and is believed to be a "sannyasin." She travels from one point to another in search of alms and begs to make a living. The body intersects Earth's orbit and descends from the Moon's tip. She resembles a serpent due to the shape of her body and is illustrated as a headless figure. The native with this conjunction in their natal chart will likely develop mental health issues. Some may even suffer from an inferiority complex or excessive jealousy. They are easily humiliated in public and are unable to accept criticism. The affiliation of the Moon with Ketu is not as healthy as other partnerships. The native lives in their own world with a frantic imagination.

While some develop mental health issues, others are susceptible to phobias. They are indecisive by nature and are rarely influenced by the positive energies or auras around them. Since the negative repercussions are only visible after a person reaches a certain age, treating the shortcomings is not an option. Astrologers suggest performing Ketu Dosha and Chandra Dosha, which are two remedies to cure the consequences. Ketu is intricately connected to past lives and spiritual energy. It can push a person into complete isolation. Getting back from that can be quite challenging, often leading to depression and eating disorders.

Moon and Mars

This pairing is quite strong and blesses the native with qualities like dynamism, prosperity, and generosity. They have good physical and mental health and rarely fall sick. If a person's natal chart depicts this affiliation, they are likely more courageous and stronger. If you are one of them, look within yourself and get in touch with your emotions, as this act can help you fight for the betterment of your family. In a way, it is also related to personal growth. However, during the native's bad days, they can easily get irritated and be more confused, especially when dealing with their emotions. This behavior is usually found in the natal charts with the Moon in transit. If you feel more irritated or agitated lately, it is time to take a step back and relax. However, if this behavior is not controlled, you can end up making bad decisions that can also affect your loved ones.

If the planets meet in an evil Nakshatra or house, the combination can transform the native's noble thoughts into dark actions. If necessary action is not taken, they can turn evil and lose direction. They may show signs of irritability, impatience, and clumsiness. Over time, they may also develop vices like alcohol abuse, womanizing, gambling, and drug abuse. This affiliation in an unfavorable house is considered worse for females as it indicates the death of a close relative.

Moon and Jupiter

Just as the conjunction of the Moon with Mars is considered to be overall favorable, the affiliation of the former with Jupiter is deemed to be noble too. The native is blessed with great physical health and loyal friends and family. They also possess creative skills and attract wealth by legal means. They are loyal to their profession and believe in hard-earned money. However, if the conjunction is afflicted, the native may suffer from a major financial loss. It can either be in the form of car accidents or a big business loss.

In some cases, the native will weigh finances over reputation and choose the latter. For them, reputation and respect stand at a higher position than financial status. If this continues over a long period, they may also loosen ties with their spouse and children.

In general, healthy conjunction keeps people more positive and encourages them to see the good in people and all circumstances. This enhances their charisma and brings them closer to others. They are admired by their friends and family too. Due to this optimistic nature, they attract positivity and can manifest favorable outcomes.

This is also the case with the Moon in transit mode. The native is content with their life and prefers to stay happy. Their good mood is infectious and can brighten other people's days. When starting a new project, they are often careful with setting intentions –another reason to gain favorable outcomes.

Moon and Saturn

This conjunction is another acknowledged affiliation that makes a person honest and clever from birth. It is called "Janma Shani Erashtaka" and is highly influential in Vedic astrology. The native who survives this phase can attract fame and wealth as they grow up. However, the native's natal chart reading can sometimes read guilt and sadness as their main qualities –particularly when the partnership is affiliated. In worst cases, they may also attract mean and abusive caretakers, which can aggravate the situation. They may struggle to find people who appreciate or value them. The need for validation and attention can hinder their emotional security. If a child fails to develop coping mechanisms to attract attention, they may fail to cope with their emotions as an adult. They may either isolate themselves or feel shy.

During the transit phase, the native may feel more distant from others, including their loved ones. Since maintaining relationships is a major task for the native, the established distance can worsen and weaken their bond. In the end, their hardship will be dictated by the inability to express emotions or feelings of rejection. Typically, women feel more prone to emotional hardships due to guilt and emotional unavailability. The native should be more open with their loved ones and work on their communication skills to overcome these issues. Failing to do so can lead to anxiety or depression.

Moon and Uranus

This pairing symbolizes uncertainty, contradiction, chaos, and unpredictability. The native experiences constant shifts in mood, which can increase irritability. They are impulsive and fail to make rational decisions which, in turn, can also affect their decision-making skills. Even though they are not fully prepared to experience change, they are always seeking variation in different domains of their life. This affiliation inspires you to see beyond the common boundaries and widen your horizons. Uranus with the Moon can easily trigger your feelings and generate conflicts. You may not only be at war with your inner self, but you may also try to unconsciously sabotage your relationships. Your behavior and personality may not align at times, which can intensify the conflict. Even though Uranus is progressive by nature and inspires the native to develop a similar attitude, the conjunction can create a conflicting pattern.

While Uranus helps the natives focus on logical and intellectual subjects, the Moon's energy can confuse and divert them towards thinking about their emotions. In most cases, they may also make emotional decisions over rational choices. This results in the conflict between the heart and the mind, which is one of the most difficult situations one faces in their life. Unfortunately, this situation gets worse if necessary steps are not taken to lighten the effects of this conjunction. The native needs a loving and emotionally stable family or loved ones to balance their emotions.

Moon and Neptune

Neptune symbolizes emotional sensitivity. Since the Moon also represents emotions, this conjunction is primarily related to one's emotional health. The native is open to all kinds of influences, which makes them more vulnerable. Your mind invites every kind of feeling, thought, emotion, slur, and suspicion. While this can provide immense knowledge up to a certain point, the inability to filter this information can lead to overthinking and emotional instability. If someone raises their voice or becomes mean, you may not be able to handle it. Over time, you may feel more isolated and prefer staying alone instead of listening to unwanted criticism. Learning some effective ways to shun negative comments and keep rejections from affecting your self-esteem is necessary. If you are born under this conjunction, you may find yourself hanging out with only a handful of people.

It is necessary to keep toxicity out of your life while learning to handle negativity. If you stay isolated for a prolonged period, you can successfully cope with negative environments or toxic people. In a way, you will rarely engage with them, which will completely eradicate the toxicity. During the Moon's transit mode, you may experience heightened confusion or brain fog, and that can impact important decisions. Every insignificant comment or argument may turn into a scandal if you allow it. Be cautious and try not to be vulnerable.

Moon and Pluto

Much like other conjunctions, this association between the Moon and Pluto also indicates an intense emotional connection. Whether you feel happy, sad, angry, or scared, all your emotions will be intensified. You feel emotions intensely and with a heavy heart. Depending on the situation, this can make you feel more grateful or push you into a downward spiral of negative emotions. You can combat this by making necessary changes to your thought process and behavioral patterns. If the issue is related to control or power, you can analyze your condition and visualize the outcome. If you hold more control or power, will the situation or issue affect you in any way? Since you have a stronghold of your feelings and emotions, use this power to turn situations in your favor.

With further improvement, you can heighten your money-making skills and polish your creative abilities to gain recognition. Once you see improvements in some areas, you may also notice a spike in your sexuality. With Pluto in place, there is no middle ground. The native may either portray obsessive-compulsive habits, control their partner, or fall victim to superiority. A proper balance needs to be established to live a long, healthy, and fulfilling life.

Moon and the Sun

One of the most powerful combinations of all, the Sun-Moon conjunction helps one feel at peace. The native has better control of their life and can exude neutral emotions that work in everyone's favor. However, they can get so diplomatic at times that it can be annoying. This can also impact their mental health. Even though the Moon and the Sun share a strong bond and thrive in harmony, their distinct energies can create an imbalance in the native's life. While the Moon is calm and emotional, the Sun is energetic and fiery. Certain zodiac signs like Aries, Leo, and Cancer support this union and make the native more confident and emotionally stable. However, as mentioned, they need to work on their diplomatic nature before it gets ingrained into their attitude.

In these cases, they may also come across as rude and arrogant, even if they don't mean to be. With the help of beneficial celestial bodies, you can deepen your knowledge and gain useful philosophical insights that can likely transform your life. On the other hand, joining hands with malefic bodies can push you into the trap of carnal desires and permanent arrogance. The idea is to become more self-aware and make an internal promise to transform your habits. Analyze whether or not your actions align with your thoughts. If not, set the right intentions and create a plan. More importantly, distinguish between your wants and needs.

Since many reliable online sources allow you to check your Moon's position with respective planets, you can easily find out more about your personality. You can also use this information to gain more consciousness and become more self-aware. If the process seems ambiguous, you can get help from a wise and experienced astrologer to illustrate minute intricacies in your natal chart. Deciphering different pairings and the union of the Moon with each planet is a great way to know yourself better and make a positive impact. Since your personality and well-being can majorly affect your loved ones, too, studying your natal chart and deciphering the Moon's location in transit can be a major step toward self-improvement and self-reflection.

Chapter 9: Lunar Phases

A lunar cycle typically consists of eight phases that can be harnessed to explore the Moon's true potential and, in turn, give you the ability to live your life to its fullest. Like a seed germinates and blooms into a flower, the Moon grows into its full form, dies, and then regenerates, marking one whole cycle. Every phase of the Moon personifies different values and innate qualities that inspire a person to regain balance and live in harmony. All eight phases are so distinct that they are visible to the naked eye. In fact, if you learn about them in detail, you can look at the sky and point out the phase that the celestial body is currently in.

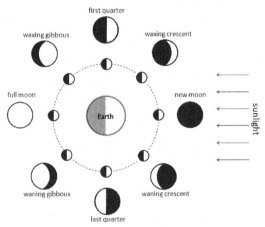

When you cannot see the Moon in a clear night sky, it may be because the moon is in its first phase. As each phase passes, the Moon enters another zodiac sign with an approximate angle of 45 degrees on the longitudinal scale. This adds up to a total of 360 degrees with eight signs on the zodiac wheel. With each phase lasting up to 3.5 days, one lunar cycle takes approximately one month to complete. While some phases gain light as they grow, others lose it, determining their respective characteristics.

First Phase- The New Moon

This phase defines the beginning of a lunar cycle where the Moon is completely invisible due to the Sun's placement. In turn, the Moon does not illuminate the Earth's face, which is why the sky appears dark. The Moon and the Sun are aligned with the Earth's face, which provides the illusion of the Moon being dark or lost in the sky. According to astrologers, both celestial bodies form a symbiosis or thrive in conjunction.

Manifestations: Just like the lunar cycle begins and motivates the Moon to grow, you should also consider setting new goals and intentions to reach closer to your goals. You can either write down your goals and break them into smaller milestones or prepare a vision board to clear your mind. Since the cycle starts on day 1 of the month, you have 29 days to accomplish your intentions. You should not only focus on starting afresh or turning over a new leaf but also on regaining your power or strength to take necessary actions. Decipher this sign to reboot your life and reinstate your energy from the Moon's power. Ideally, this phase represents birth and the steady growth phase that follows as a person grows up.

Typically, a person born in this phase possesses childlike traits. They are full of life, enthusiastic, and ready to take charge. Just like a seed is implanted underground and gets optimum nutrition to burst out and bloom into a flower, this phase encourages you to unleash your true potential and start a new project. Note that over-enthusiasm can often ruin the process, thereby affecting the outcome. It is necessary to comprehend the practical concerns while listening to your gut to achieve favorable outcomes. Stay courageous and shun the peers who put you down. Gather your energy and focus on one thing instead of scattering yourself in multiple places.

Consider this phase a new beginning and an inspiration to promote growth in your personal and professional life. Whether you are having trouble sustaining your relationships or facing work issues, chart out your concerns and set intentions to combat your shortcomings. While vision boards and goal-setting approaches are some effective techniques to set your intentions, you should also focus on chanting positive affirmations every day to see better results. Discard all negative thoughts and make room for positive notions. Let go of the past and learn from your mistakes. If you have held a desire in your heart and mind for a while, consider this as a sign to put it into action.

Second Phase- The Waxing Moon (Crescent)

In its second phase, the Moon appears in a crescent shape due to the Sun's slight movement. However, since the Sun still covers a major part of the Moon, the latter appears as a thin silver lining. The waxing moon signifies building energy and the buried seed that is slowly gaining strength to sprout.

Manifestations: Just like the Moon slowly powers up to retain its shape, you should also work on your inner strength and qualities to boost self-confidence and reach your goals. Other qualities like self-assurance, self-esteem, and compassion should also be polished. Take time to plan out your actions and take inspiration from the crescent moon to move ahead. You can set your own pace and take one step at a time. The idea is to keep moving irrespective of the speed or the pace you pick. Since you have already set your intentions during the first phase, it is time to take the first step by gaining inspiration from the crescent moon. Those born under the second phase of the Moon know that there is more to life and that new adventures await ahead.

Third Phase- The First Quarter (Waxing)

The third Phase (or "waxing") is when the Moon appears sliced in half due to the Sun's coverage. It can take up to one week for the Moon to reach the third phase and display its face in half. Since the Moon completes one-fourth of a lunar cycle, this phase is also known as the First Quarter. At this point, the Moon is in waxing mode.

Manifestations: This phase asks a person to take a break and reflect on their intentions. It emphasizes the importance of pausing and reveling in your life. Take a look at your plans and comprehend whether or not you are going in the right direction. This will keep you from making irreversible mistakes and avoid adverse repercussions. This phase also signifies action and the need to pull yourself from external resistances. While pausing and reflecting on your intentions is necessary, knowing the right way to move ahead is important too. If you are sure about your path, you must put yourself in full gear and take charge.

At this point, the buried seed has sprouted and made its way above ground to turn into a small sapling. Even though it is not fully grown yet, the sapling is absorbing the Sun's energy for optimum growth. However, it needs the will and courage to sustain itself regardless of external forces until it grows into a strong tree that bare hands cannot uproot. Similarly, a person born under this phase is confident, passionate, and willing to take risks. However, they must combat all the challenges and hardships coming their way. They must be quick on their feet and motivated. Since these people have a lot of courage and determination, they often carve their path by taking action under any circumstances.

Fourth Phase- The Waxing Gibbous Moon

The fourth phase reveals a major part of the Moon's surface and is just one step away from transforming into a Full Moon. This phase illuminates the sky and the Earth's surface and is also visible during the daytime. The Sun covers only one-fourth of the Moon.

Manifestations: This phase declares that you are just one step away from fulfilling your goal. You just need a little push and some commitment to achieve what you set out to do. However, you must also be mindful and pay attention to the tiniest details to avoid losing track of time. At the same time, focus on honing your skills to create an edge over your competitors. This phase also keeps you aware and asks you to look back and redesign your action plan if it seems bleak. This is the step where you have to take your goals extremely seriously and put in your best effort to achieve them.

The sapling starts bearing buds at this point, and you can notice tiny fruits ready to sprout. Just like the plant is preparing itself to bear fruits until they are ready to be picked, you also have to take care of your actions and emotions until you reach your final destination. You need proper organization and planning skills to ease the burden. It is also necessary to acknowledge your thoughts and emotions to judge your current condition and lead a peaceful life while getting closer to your ambition.

People born under this phase are naturally curious. In essence, they want to know more about themselves and their life's purpose. If they feel they lack in some way, they instantly seek personal development and find ways to express themselves. While self-analysis is a part of their daily lives, they also watch others around them and acknowledge their usefulness. Since they constantly need motivation, they will likely keep away from people who fail to inspire them.

Fifth Phase- The Full Moon

At this point, the Moon and the Sun stand in opposite directions, leading to portraying a full version of the Moon and allowing it to shine brightly, sending as much light as possible to Earth's surface. The Full Moon symbolizes the completion of a cycle and the urge to start a new chapter. By tapping into this overflowing energy, you can strengthen your intentions and find solutions to your problems.

Manifestations: Even though both celestial bodies are at opposite ends, a person may find it difficult to strike a balance due to the elevated tension. You may feel overwhelmed because of the deluge of emotions. On the bright side, look at the Full Moon as an opportunity to shine bright and reveal your true inner self. If you are successful, you may even find your inner calling. To tap into the Full Moon's true side, you can resort to several tricks and rituals such as crystal healing, meditations, and spell chanting. Be wary of overflowing emotions as they can ruin the entire process and invalidate all your hard work.

The seed you sowed during the first phase has completely bloomed and is bearing fruits at this point. It is ready to be fully expressed and to allow its fruits to be harvested. Just like the Sun and the Moon stand staring at each other in awe, individuals influenced by this phase often seek partners who admire them. Typically, these people are blessed with fulfilled lives and thrive in peace. The Full Moon implies the need and desire of having a loving partner who completes the seeker. Before they find their spouse or soulmate, these people will learn about harmonious engagement in their personal and professional lives. They are blessed to experience varied and interesting adventures throughout their journey.

Sixth Phase- The Waning Gibbous Moon (Disseminating)

The Moon is partially covered by the Sun to the right side during this phase, which forms a mirror image of the Waxing Moon. This form of the body is known as the Waning Gibbous Moon and portrays diminishing powers. The Sun partly creates a shadow on the Moon, slowly heading towards its last quarter version.

Manifestations: This is the step where you take a break again and reflect on your journey. Comprehend your path and acknowledge how far you have come. This is the time to review and assess your progress. If you still feel like changing certain things to accomplish your goals with ease, take a step back and reiterate your plan. At the same time, you should feel grateful to have come this far. All the hard work and time invested is paying off. Take a moment to thank your loved ones and the people who helped you during this journey. Even if you haven't accomplished all your intentions so far, you may still see one of your small goals being fulfilled. At this point, you wish to give back the wisdom and possessions you acquired to date.

Individuals born under this phase are naturally enthusiastic and know how to enjoy their lives regardless of circumstances. The flowers and fruit on the plant are fading at this point. The seeds are falling on the ground and ready to be buried again. The term "disseminating" refers to falling off and giving back. Just like the tree returns the seeds to the Earth to restart the cycle, you should also give away love, laughter, and wisdom to people around you. As well as this, individuals capable of succeeding will find an easier path to accomplish their goals.

Seventh Phase- The Third Quarter (Last Quarter or Waning)

This phase of the Moon is the mirror image of the First Quarter, covered in half by the Sun's shadow. The Moon shines on the left side as opposed to the right side during the First Quarter. It is reaching the last phase of fading away from the night sky.

Manifestations: If you are holding back your emotions or being held back due to some form of negativity, it is time to let go of your gloomy thoughts. Believe in yourself and know your worth. Negative thoughts, along with any kind of fear or self-limiting beliefs, should be discarded. While it is easier said than done, giving up is not an option at this stage. You can seek professional help or lean on your loved ones to combat fear and negative emotions. If you are holding onto the feelings or possessions that are not serving you in any positive way, release them and cleanse your system.

Forgive those who hurt you and begin to seek solitude. Leave your emotional baggage behind before moving forward. Work on your anger and do not regret following your dream. Move ahead with a light heart and mind. The tree you planted is losing its leaves and colors. It has entered the fall season and is embracing the change. People representing this phase constantly reanalyze their situation and redesign old patterns to achieve a better outcome.

Eight Phase- The Dark Moon (Balsamic)

The Sun is dominant over the Moon and covers a major part of its surface at this point. You can only see a thin crescent-shaped illuminating body during this last phase. The Moon is about to fade and give way to the invisible New Moon.

Manifestations: You may or may not have reached your goal or fulfilled your intentions. Irrespective of the outcome, you should reflect on your journey and examine your condition. It is the moment to take pride in yourself and pat yourself on the shoulder. Remember that you cannot control everything, and you are just in the right place. Even if you haven't fulfilled your goals, consider your past mistakes and work out the steps to change. Get inspired and motivate others too. Surrendering to the universe's power will give you peace and propel your actions.

Let fate drive your vehicle and get excited for the new beginnings as you enter a new life cycle. Even though this cycle represents death, it is still an invitation for rebirth or regeneration. The tree you planted is completely dead now but is preparing itself for spring. The fallen seeds are hibernating inside the ground and preparing themselves for the next cycle to begin. You may find it easier to leave others behind and accept your circumstances if born under this phase. You believe in completion and reinstating a new journey. You prefer to spend time alone rather than being with the wrong people.

The next phase is the New Moon, where it completely disappears and marks the beginning of a new cycle. In essence, a lunar cycle is a natural example of a cycle representing birth, death, and regeneration. While the new moon refers to the beginning of a life cycle and setting relevant intentions, the full moon depicts completion, death, or an ending.

It is believed that following the Moon's phases and inculcating relevant values can truly change a person's life. In a way, the Moon gives us signs and wisdom to manifest positive changes to our routines and helps us to become more self-aware. Pay attention to each phase and decipher the innate tone each element carries. Compare your zodiac sign with the phase you were born in to comprehend your emotions and intuition. By digging deeper, you may also find your true purpose or calling in life. To find your birth phase, compare your Sun and Moon signs and count the difference in their placements. The number you get is the Moon phase you were born in.

Chapter 10: Harness the Magic of the Moon

Moon magic and tantras have been a significant part of astrology for ages. The Moon has impacted the gravitational pull and the movement of tides and has acted as a guide for farmers and hunters to grow their crops based on the best seasonal and climatic conditions. However, the Moon has not always been in favor of all living creatures on Earth. While some are blessed with the Moon's valediction, others need to harness the body's power and energy to get better outcomes. While Moon magic was more relevant to ancient scholars and magicians, you can still practice some routines at home too.

Why Are Spells and Rituals Important for the Moon?

As you learned, the spiritual and mythological importance of the Moon can be unraveled by performing certain spells and following some effective methods to please the celestial body. Moon magic and rituals were an integral part of Chinese, Egyptian, and Indian culture in the past. They were considered sacred and pivotal ways to recharge and carry out normal day-to-day activities. Since some cultures still follow lunar calendars and cycles to mark time and dates, channeling the Moon's energy to validate your feelings can be a vital step towards self-improvement.

Every phase of a lunar cycle helps you develop in different areas. For instance, while some seek a productivity boost through spells and rituals, others need insights into inner contemplation and self-care. In a way, the rituals are a screen to absorb in self-reflection and take charge of your personal and professional life. Moon rituals, in particular, send an invite to feel silent and peaceful on the inside. To combat growing despair and challenges, you need to plant some intentions within your mind and follow the lunar phases. This will also make you more committed and provide a definite path to follow with immense focus and perseverance.

Routines and Rituals for Each Moon Phase

Even though we learned about the moon phases of a lunar cycle in the previous chapter, we will recall them here to understand the best ritual or routine to please the Moon at each step. Here are some effective routines and rituals you should perform during each moon phase to harness the magical power of the Moon and feel at peace.

First Phase- New Moon

Your Focus: The first step is to set intentions. Just as the Moon is ready to be born and start its journey, you need to set your goals and illustrate your journey. What do you want to achieve in life? What are the areas you want to improve? Do you see yourself at a specific place after a few years?

Ritual: Since this phase aligns with the idea of stepping into new beginnings, you need a routine that can help with goal-setting and deciphering your thoughts. Journaling is an effective way to clear your mind and begin to design your goals. It also paves a path for introspection and provides the assurance of leading the path.

How to Perform: Buy a bullet journal or make your diary with paper scraps to write your daily thoughts and clarify your vision. To set your goals, you must first learn to read your mind. Are there any areas of your life currently bothering you? Write them down. It could be your career, personal relationships, or even a new project you meant to begin. Chart them out and visualize your goals.

Now, write "New Moon Intentions" on the first blank page along with the date. You can also add pictures or doodles to recognize your concerns or desires. You must practice this routine every day for at least 15 to 30 minutes for effective results. When writing in your journal, create a sacred or clutter-free space to get clearer thoughts. Light a candle and take deep breaths to feel at ease. Set five core intentions and jot them down in bullet points on paper when you are ready to start. Use the present tense and address your intentions in the first person to believe that they are already in action. Read and repeat your intentions out loud and visualize them in real life while closing your eyes.

Second Phase- Waxing Crescent Moon

Your Focus: During this phase, the Moon starts showing itself in the sky, which indicates that it is time to take action. At this point, you should have an action plan ready to start following it. Even if it is a small step, start moving ahead to fulfill your intentions. While leaping is vital to achieving success, you should also learn how to nurture your ideas and heighten your self-esteem.

Ritual: You can take help from some powerful spells or mantras to grow your career or strengthen your personal relationships. Reflect on the intentions you set during the Moon's first phase and cast spells based on the area of improvement. When casting the spells, it is necessary to visualize and think that you have already achieved your goal.

How to Perform: Let's say that your main intention is to find a new job and excel in your career. You can resort to a spell that is further narrowed down and specifically based on your professional goal. For example, if you are looking for a new job, you can cast a spell related to "Demeter & Ceres." On the other hand, casting a Wiccan bath spell will help you have a successful interview. You can alter your spells based on your intentions. If your goal is to find a partner, you have to cast a different set of spells using the same method.

Third Phase- First Quarter

Your Focus: This is the stage when you take action and implement the plan with full force. However, you need clarity to ensure that you are moving in the right direction. Get attuned with your body's natural movement and your thought process. When both are in harmony, you can achieve all your goals.

Ritual: This can be fulfilled by performing a set of breathing exercises specifically meant for the First Quarter phase of a lunar cycle. You can also perform meditation and synchronize your emotions with your actions.

How to Perform: Find a quiet space where you can peacefully perform meditation. Sit cross-legged and play calming music. Close your eyes and clear your mind. If any thought crosses your mind, shift your focus to your breathing pattern. Take deep breaths and keep your focus intact. Perform a breathing exercise called "kumbhaka," where you inhale and hold the same amount of breath but let out double the amount. Since it can take some time to master breathing techniques and meditation, you must be patient.

Fourth Phase- Waxing Gibbous

Your Focus: The Moon is steadily growing and is ready to transform into a Full Moon version. It acts as a fuel to recharge and inspires you to keep expanding and growing. You are putting your maximum effort toward fulfilling your intentions. If you are feeling tired or demotivated, take inspiration from the Waxing Gibbous Moon.

Ritual: Known as the "Intuitive Oracle," this ritual is based on referring to a deck of oracle cards to nurture your actions. Ideally, oracle cards are used to read and interpret your perspective on specific steps you are currently undertaking. Some even use a set to enhance self-awareness and become more intuitive.

How to Perform: When choosing a set of oracle cards, focus on the theme and your intuition. Pick the card that calls out to you. You can also collect several decks and use one based on your current circumstances or mood. Before you shuffle the cards, take a deep breath and clear your mind. Recall your intentions while you are shuffling the cards. Lay them on a flat surface and spread them out evenly.

Now, use your left hand and hover it over the cards at a steady pace. Pause at the card that pulls and draws you in the most. Once you feel this pull, draw two random cards and place them upside down. The first card will declare your main intention, and the second card will validate your action. If you are not on the right path, it is time to change your course.

At the same time, take a pause and analyze your plan again. Make the necessary changes before moving ahead. You must be at the top of your game by this stage, as it will determine whether or not you will achieve favorable outcomes. This ritual will also help you overcome hurdles, combat shortcomings, and nurture new thoughts and ideas.

Fifth Phase- Full Moon

Your Focus: At this point, the Moon grows into a full circle and marks completion. It refers to a phase where you are seeking abundance or have undergone a complete transformation. Practice gratefulness, thank yourself, and acknowledge your journey. Plan around your Full Moon days to perform cleansing and purifying rituals.

Ritual: You need to let go of negativity by writing down all the things bothering you and burning the piece of paper. Watch the paper burn and visualize your negative thoughts vanishing into the flames. You can also take a Moon bath to integrate the celestial body's energy with water. This ritual provokes feelings and unlocks emotional intelligence, which is ideal during the Full Moon phase. With this, you can also decipher the Moon's musings and comprehend the emotions it is trying to evoke.

How to Perform: To prepare your bath, mix 1/4 cup of Himalayan pink salt with 1/2 cup of Epsom salt. Next, you need an essential oil to act as a carrier. You can use lavender, frankincense, jasmine, chamomile, or sweet almond essential oil. Add 2 to 3 drops to the salt mixture. To enhance the mixture's effect, add a few flower petals for an invigorating effect. It is time to prepare your bathtub. Fill it with water and add the salt and essential oil mixture. Dim the lights and light scented candles for a relaxing effect.

When taking a bath, let the water touch your skin and take deep breaths to get into a meditative state. Feel your physical presence and let go of all worries. Remember, this is the time to feel grateful for your existence and your body. As you become more mindful when taking a bath, you will also feel more connected to your mind and soul. At the same time, recall your intentions and start visualizing them. Whether you are looking for a compatible partner or finding a new career choice, imagine yourself in a positive light while letting the water cleanse your soul and mind. Believe that you are destined to achieve positive outcomes.

Once you have finished taking a bath, let the water drain along with your negative thoughts. You are not done yet. After your bath, rub some body oil all over your arms, legs, stomach, chest, back, and neck. To make this routine more effective, play calming music, light incense sticks, or create an ambiance that will heighten your senses.

Irrespective of your gender, this routine will help you unravel your feminine side and explore your sexual energy, one of a human being's purest and most vulnerable sides.

You can also take this time to charge your crystals and energize them using the Moon's full power. Place your crystals at a dry and dust-free spot under the moonlight for 48 hours. The best spot is your windowsill, as you can keep an eye on your crystals while they are recharging. Even though you can keep your crystals for just a few hours, astrologers suggest leaving them for at least two nights to soak up maximum cosmic energy.

Sixth Phase- Waning Gibbous

Your Focus: As the Moon starts to fade slowly due to the Sun's coverage over its surface, you should take a step back and reflect on your journey too. The work you have done so far should be validated and appreciated.

Ritual: You can use the Moon's energy (which is still high until it reaches the next phase) to charge any liquid and make "Moon water." People usually use drinking water to make this sacred potion. You can either drink it, apply it to your body, or spray it around your house to get the most out of the Moon's energy. Some even incorporate it into their beauty routine.

How to Perform: To make Moon water, you need one cup of distilled water and a glass jar or bottle. Pour the water into the jar and place it under the moonlight for two days. Make sure to set and recall your intentions when following this ritual. For an enhanced effect, write your intentions down and place the piece of paper near the glass jar. Add your Moon water to your beverages, sip it directly from the bottle, or use it in your skincare routine after mixing it with a few drops of essential oil. When using it, repeat and visualize your intentions.

Seventh Phase- Third Quarter

Your Focus: This is the stage where you let go of the bothersome thoughts and combat stagnation. Just like the First Quarter Moon inspired you to start a new project or relationship, the Third Quarter Moon asks you to let go of the things that didn't work out.

Ritual: At this stage, you can perform exercises related to movement. It could be yoga, dance, or any other movement form inspired by the Moon's flow.

How to Perform: The Moon dance is a popular ritual that many cultures have followed for centuries. Even though it is typically performed on a New Moon or Full Moon day, some prefer to dance during other lunar phases. While some simply move around chanting Moon mantras, others gather in a big circle and perform the Moon dance. "Lightning walking" is another movement exercise where you walk around with heavy feet. This act resembles stomping but feels like a lightning strike. This helps your body release all stagnant energy and gives you fresh power to move to the next phase without any regrets. Any kind of movement will release accumulated negative energy and make room for a more positive aura.

Eight Phase- Waning Crescent Moon

Your Focus: Just like the Sun covers a major part of the Moon's surface to achieve completion, you should also reflect on your journey and analyze your mistakes to learn from them. This is the time to take a pause and contemplate how far you have come. Even if you haven't achieved success or are far away from your goals, you can restart the journey after taking a brief pause. If it seems overwhelming, note that it is okay to surrender. You can withdraw and relax.

Ritual: A clean and clutter-free environment will help you think clearly and bring you peace. The ritual is called "clutter cleanse," where you discard all the unnecessary items in your living space and make your life more pleasant.

How to Perform: Start by making a list of all the unwanted items and possessions in your home. While experts suggest focusing on just one space that you often use to work or sleep in, you can gradually declutter your entire home and feel more energized. Collect and sort all the objects based on their size, nature, and usefulness. If you haven't used a particular item for over a year, discard it. Do not hoard unnecessary stuff. In a way, this will also improve your decision-making skills, which are necessary to develop a clear mind. You can either sell the items or donate them to people in need.

By doing this, you are creating a sacred space for your body and mind. Over time, you will also notice a boost in your confidence and energy levels. Decluttering your living space is not just useful for your mind and soul, but it also reduces the effort you need to put into cleaning. It also enhances your home's aesthetic appeal and makes the spaces look bigger. Your sacred sanctuary is now ready. You can light candles, introduce a pleasant fragrance, or play music to make the spaces more peaceful. Use this new space to meditate every day.

Note that these rituals and routines will take some time to show positive results. Keep performing them over and over again, and you will soon see their benefits as a few cycles pass. Until then, believe in your intentions and focus on your actions.

Conclusion

Before you started reading this book, you may have had a different perspective on the relevance and existence of the Moon in the solar system. While some are aware of this natural body's importance in the world of astrology, others do not regard its prevalence as much as they should. Whether you are a pagan who wants to dig deeper into the astrological realm or a beginner simply dipping their toes in this, implementing the things in this book can help you mold the next chapter of your life. You can go back and refer to the practical guide that teaches the right way to perform magic and rituals to impact a positive change.

Let's cite the notions we've learned so far. The Moon has been perceived as a goddess for centuries and still holds significant implications in various cultures. Even though the illustration and depiction of the Lunar gods are different in all mythologies, the collective attributes depict the Moon Goddess as a dominant force symbolizing fertility and femininity. In the past, devotees made several sacrifices to please the deity, who, in turn, blessed them with wisdom and fertility.

Analyzing your moon sign does not only help you summon your emotions, but it also strengthens your relationship with the important women in your life. The Moon primarily rules over the Cancer zodiac sign and is related to womanhood, fertility, and security signs. The Moon signs govern different emotions and sides of every individual. For instance, while the Capricorn is ambitious and willing to work harder due to the weaker Moon sign, the Taurus glorifies the orbiting energy.

By knowing your place, time, and date of birth, you can easily determine your Moon sign and connect it to your zodiac sign. While some signs can freely express their thoughts and are emotionally available for their partners, others are more reserved and prefer to stay isolated. Furthermore, the Lunar South Node (Ketu) and North Node (Rahu) define the imperfect characteristics possessed by each individual, which are either excessively developed or stand below the usual standard, respectively. Since both nodes stand opposite each other, they depict karmic imbalance. The correlation of the Moon with other planets is quite versatile. While it thrives in harmony with some planets, the natural body creates negative conjunction (contrasts) with other celestial bodies.

The Lunar phases can also be studied to understand the natural cyclical events that can, in a way, govern your life and help you decipher your feelings. As the cycle of life begins from birth, the first phase marks the beginning of any process. As the Moon portrays different forms with each passing phase, it inspires you to set intentions, move ahead, reflect on your mistakes, and inspire others. In a way, it marks the birth and death of any process while signifying the importance of regeneration or rebirth. Every process that ends has a new beginning.

The right way to manifest the Moon's true energy is by performing effective rituals and magic. You can either chant positive affirmations, use crystals, or perform a moon bath to stay attuned with its energy. Recall the other robust ways to perform moon magic discussed in the last chapter.

That's the power of the Moon. You can simply bask under the powerful illumination and feel energized or read the Moon's placement to manifest positive change in your life and find your true self. Now that you have acquired complete knowledge about the Moon's role in astrology, take the leap and use the orbiting body's power to reap maximum benefits. Use this book as an inspiration to change your life and motivate others around you.

Good luck embodying the relevance of "la luna" and "know thyself"!

Here's another book by Mari Silva that you might like

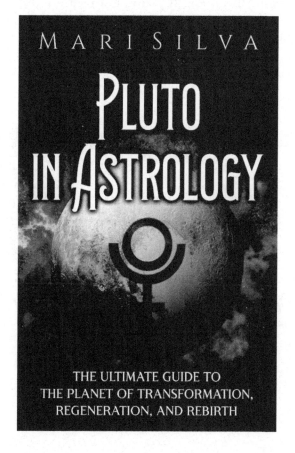

Your Free Gift (only available for a limited time)

Thanks for getting this book! If you want to learn more about various spirituality topics, then join Mari Silva's community and get a free guided meditation MP3 for awakening your third eye. This guided meditation mp3 is designed to open and strengthen ones third eye so you can experience a higher state of consciousness. Simply visit the link below the image to get started.

https://spiritualityspot.com/meditation

References

Mack, L. (2021, January 12). How to understand your moon sign. Retrieved from Thecut.com website: https://www.thecut.com/article/moon-sign-astrology-what-your-moon-sign-means.html

The Moon. (n.d.). Retrieved from Astrology-zodiac-signs.com website: https://www.astrology-zodiac-signs.com/astrology/planets/moon/

A Wiccan Guide to Moon magic – Wicca living. (2017, June 16). Retrieved from Wiccaliving.com website: https://wiccaliving.com/wiccan-full-moon-ritual/

Chang'e – Chinese goddess of the moon. (2021, July 1). Retrieved from Symbolsage.com website: https://symbolsage.com/chinese-goddess-of-the-moon/

Luna - Roman goddess of the moon - symbol sage. (2020, December 2). Retrieved from Symbolsage.com website: https://symbolsage.com/luna-roman-moon-goddess/

MacDougal, C. (2019, December 9). How the Moon affects us. Retrieved from Athrbeauty.com website: https://athrbeauty.com/blogs/goodvibesbeauty/how-the-moon-its-phases-affect-us

Selene – the Greek moon goddess. (2020, December 14). Retrieved from Symbolsage.com website: https://symbolsage.com/selene-greek-moon-goddess/

Sin (mythology). (n.d.). Retrieved from Newworldencyclopedia.org website: https://www.newworldencyclopedia.org/entry/Sin_(mythology)

The legend of Chang E. (n.d.). Retrieved from Moonfestival.org website: http://www.moonfestival.org/the-legend-of-chang-e.html

Thompson, A. (2009, October 5). Our changing view of the moon. Retrieved from Space website: https://www.space.com/7338-changing-view-moon.html

Thoth -the Egyptian god of wisdom and writing. (2020, October 20). Retrieved from Symbolsage.com website: https://symbolsage.com/thoth-egyptian-god-of-wisdom/

Who is Chandra the Hindu god? (2013, February 13). Retrieved from Synonym.com website: https://classroom.synonym.com/who-is-chandra-the-hindu-god-12086016.html

Yanka. (n.d.). Chandra or Moon God – born from the ocean of the mind. Retrieved from Sagarworld.com website: https://www.sagarworld.com/ramayan/chandra-or-moon-god-born-from-the-ocean-of-the-mind

astrosharmistha. (2019, September 19). Moon in Vedic Astrology -. Retrieved from Astrosharmistha.com website: http://astrosharmistha.com/blog/moon-in-vedic-astrology/

Bhattacharjee, A. S. (2018, June 18). Moon Remedies Astrology For Weak, Debilitated, Afflicted, combusted state. Retrieved from Astrosanhita.com website: https://astrosanhita.com/remedies-for-weak-debilitated-afflicted-moon-in-astrology/

HeereJawharat.com. (2015, June). Retrieved from Heerejawharat.com website: https://www.heerejawharat.com/gemstones-astrology-significance/white-pearl-astrological-significance.php

Moon Nakshatra: Your Vedic Moon Sign. (2018, July 25). Retrieved from Serenityspaonline.com website: https://serenityspaonline.com/moon-nakshatra-sign/

Prusty, M. (2019, January 23). Role and importance of Moon in Vedic astrology. Retrieved from Astroguruonline.com website: https://www.astroguruonline.com/importance-moon-vedic-astrology/

Rocks, D. (2013, October 25). Moon in Cancer: Characteristics and personality traits. Retrieved from Com.au website: https://www.starslikeyou.com.au/your-astrology-profile/moon-in-cancer/

Speaks, J. (2020, January 29). 10 best home remedies for Moon planet in males & females horoscope. Retrieved from Jupiterspeaks.com website: https://jupiterspeaks.com/general-remedies-problems-related-planet-moon/

Vani, A. (2013, August 5). How to make your Moon stronger - remedies by Pawan Sinha. Retrieved from Astro-vani.com website: https://www.astro-vani.com/blog/make-your-moon-balanced/

Hall, M. (n.d.). What It Means When the Moon is in Taurus. Retrieved from Liveabout.com website: https://www.liveabout.com/when-the-moon-is-in-taurus-207337

Rocks, D. (2013a, October 25). Moon in Cancer: Characteristics and personality traits. Retrieved from Com.au website: https://www.starslikeyou.com.au/your-astrology-profile/moon-in-cancer/

Rocks, D. (2013b, October 25). Moon in Gemini. Retrieved from Com.au website: https://www.starslikeyou.com.au/your-astrology-profile/moon-in-gemini/

Rocks, D. (2013c, October 25). The Moon in Aries: Characteristics and personality traits. Retrieved from Com.au website: https://www.starslikeyou.com.au/your-astrology-profile/the-moon-in-aries/

Libra Moon. (n.d.). Retrieved from Justastrologythings.com website: https://justastrologythings.com/pages/planets/moon/libra.php

Matsumoto, A. (2020, April 2). Moon in Scorpio: Recognize true value and seize it all. Retrieved from Keikopowerwish.com website: https://www.keikopowerwish.com/blog/moon-in-scorpio-recognize-true-value-and-seize-it-all

Moon in Leo: 5 strengths & 5 challenges of the natal Moon in Leo. (n.d.). Retrieved from https://popularastrology.com/leo-moon

Moon in Virgo. (2016, November 29). Retrieved from Ganeshaspeaks.com website: https://www.ganeshaspeaks.com/zodiac-signs/virgo/moon-in-virgo/

What is your Moon sign, and what does it say about you? (2021, May 23). Retrieved from Russh.com website: https://www.russh.com/what-is-your-moon-sign/

Faragher, A. K. (2018, April 23). What your moon sign says about your emotional personality. Retrieved from Allure website: https://www.allure.com/story/zodiac-moon-sign-emotional-personality

jracioppi. (2013, March 11). New Moon in Pisces. Retrieved from Jenniferracioppi.com website: https://jenniferracioppi.com/new-moon-in-pisces/

Moon in Aquarius sign: Meaning, significance and personality traits. (2014, September 17). Retrieved from Sunsigns.org website: https://www.sunsigns.org/moon-in-aquarius/

Moon in Sagittarius. (n.d.). Retrieved from Lunaf.com website: https://lunaf.com/astrology/moon-in-zodiac/sagittarius/

Admin, D. (2019, August 24). Understanding your lunar south node (AKA karma). Retrieved from Dooznyc.com website: https://dooznyc.com/blogs/the-scope/understanding-your-lunar-south-node-aka-karma

Backlund, R. (2018, April 18). This piece of your birth chart reveals the parts of yourself you're meant to leave behind. Retrieved from Elitedaily.com website: https://www.elitedaily.com/p/what-does-your-south-node-mean-in-astrology-what-it-says-about-the-obstacles-youre-meant-to-overcome-8814403

McKinley, E. (2021, February 20). South node astrology and past life karma. Retrieved from Ouiwegirl.com website: https://www.ouiwegirl.com/astrology/2021/2/20/southnodeastrology

AstroTwins. (2013, October 19). North nodes & south nodes: The astrology of your life purpose and past lives. Retrieved from Astrostyle.com website: https://astrostyle.com/learn-astrology/north-south-nodes/

Fosu, K. (2020, November 3). Astrology: An easy guide to understanding the north node in the birth chart. Retrieved from Mystic Minds website: https://medium.com/mystic-minds/astrology-an-easy-guide-to-understanding-the-role-of-the-north-node-in-the-chart-e1f998bb555a

Johnson, E. (n.d.). Understanding your north node. Retrieved from Zennedout.com website: https://zennedout.com/understanding-your-north-node/

Astrolada. (n.d.). Astrolada. Retrieved from Astrolada.com website: https://www.astrolada.com/articles/planets-in-aspects/moon-with-rahu-in-the-horoscope.html

Carter, J. (2020a, January 2). Moon conjunct Mars natal and transit: New initiatives. Retrieved from Horoscopejoy.com website: https://www.horoscopejoy.com/moon-conjunct-mars-natal-and-transit-new-initiatives/

Carter, J. (2020b, January 2). Moon conjunct Uranus natal and transit: Unexpected opportunities. Retrieved from Horoscopejoy.com website: https://www.horoscopejoy.com/moon-conjunct-uranus-natal-and-transit-unexpected-opportunities/

Partridge, J. (2014, May 8). Moon conjunct Saturn natal and transit – Astrology King. Retrieved from Astrologyking.com website: https://astrologyking.com/moon-conjunct-saturn/

Partridge, J. (2015, April 30). Moon conjunct Mercury natal and transit – astrology king. Retrieved from Astrologyking.com website: https://astrologyking.com/moon-conjunct-mercury/

Partridge, J. (2017a, January 29). Moon conjunct Venus natal and transit – astrology king. Retrieved from Astrologyking.com website: https://astrologyking.com/moon-conjunct-venus/

Partridge, J. (2017b, February 28). Moon conjunct Neptune natal and transit – astrology king. Retrieved from Astrologyking.com website: https://astrologyking.com/moon-conjunct-neptune/

Patchirajan, A. (2017, September 19). Moon & Ketu conjunction. Retrieved from Cosmicinsights.net website: https://blog.cosmicinsights.net/moon-ketu-conjuction/

The Transit Moon. (n.d.). Retrieved from Thedarkpixieastrology.com website: http://www.thedarkpixieastrology.com/the-transit-moon.html

Today, C. (2020, May 23). Planetary conjunctions - DWI-graha samyoga: Moon conjunct with other planets. Retrieved from Ceylon Today website:

https://ceylontoday.lk/news/planetary-conjunctions-dwi-graha-samyoga-moon-conjunct-with-other-planets

Crawford, C. (2019, October 21). Moon phases and their meanings — the self-care emporium. Retrieved from Theselfcareemporium.com website: https://theselfcareemporium.com/blog/moon-phases-and-their-meanings

Grabarczyk, J. (2019, November 19). Your quick guide to moon phases, their meaning, and how they impact you. Retrieved from Yogiapproved.com website: https://www.yogiapproved.com/life/moon-phases-meanings-impact/

Martin, L., & Backlund, R. (2017, October 4). How to use each phase of the moon to lead A smarter, more creative life. Retrieved from Elitedaily.com website: https://www.elitedaily.com/lifestyle/moon-phases-affects-body-mind

Eaton, A. (2020, April 10). Moon ritual practices for every lunar phase — oui we. Retrieved from Ouiwegirl.com website: https://www.ouiwegirl.com/beauty/2020/4/8/moon-rituals

Garis, M. G. (2021, March 18). How to take a ritual moon bath and bring forth your wildest dreams. Retrieved from Well+Good website: https://www.wellandgood.com/moon-bath-ritual/

How to align with the four phases of the moon. (2020, February 14). Retrieved from Goop.com website: https://goop.com/wellness/spirituality/how-to-align-with-the-moon/

Hurst, K. (2017, March 23). Simple moon rituals for abundance to enhance manifestation. Retrieved from Thelawofattraction.com website: https://www.thelawofattraction.com/manifestation-rituals-phase-moon/

jracioppi. (2018, March 15). Moon rituals: How to manifest with the moon. Retrieved from Jenniferracioppi.com website: https://jenniferracioppi.com/moon-rituals-how-to-manifest-with-the-moon/

Moon Rituals for guiding intentions. (n.d.). Retrieved from Kelleemaize.com website: https://www.kelleemaize.com/post/moon-rituals-for-guiding-intentions

Stokes, V. (2021, July 30). How to make your own moon water: Origins, lore, and DIY ritual. Retrieved from Healthline.com website: https://www.healthline.com/health/moon-water

Made in the USA
Coppell, TX
11 November 2021